A Retreat With
Our Lady, Dominic and Ignatius

Praying With Our Bodies

Betsey Beckman, Nina O'Connor
and J. Michael Sparough, S.J.

ST. ANTHONY MESSENGER PRESS

Cincinnati, Ohio

Other titles in the
A Retreat With... *Series:*

Cover illustrations by Steve Erspamer, S.M.
Cover and book design by Mary Alfieri
Electronic format and pagination by Sandra Digman

ISBN 0-86716-256-2

Published by St. Anthony Messenger Press
Printed in the U.S.A.

Contents

For all those Mentors
who have taught us
how to pray
with more than words

Acknowledgments

We thank the many people who have worked with us and prayed for us during the birthing of this book. We especially thank the following midwives: Mary Bloom, Pat Dorian, Jean Masterson, C.S.J., Felicia McKnight, Karen Nemec, Roberta Nobleman, the Rosa Mystica Prayer Group, Celeste Snowber Schroeder, Bob Sears, S.J., Tom Sparough, Tria Thompson and Lisa von Stamwitz.

We acknowledge a special debt of gratitude to Margaret Higgins for the many, many hours she spent helping us with the manuscript. We also thank her son, Graham, for sharing his mother's time with us.

Our series editor, Gloria Hutchinson, has been a special joy to work with. Her patient pen, sharp scissors and long-distance glasses have served us well in this process.

We also thank Charlie and Chaz and all our families, the Springfield Dominicans and the Jesuit Community at Bellarmine Hall for loving us through this labor!

Introducing A Retreat With...

Twenty years ago I made a weekend retreat at a Franciscan house on the coast of New Hampshire. The retreat director's opening talk was as lively as a long-range weather forecast. He told us how completely God loves each one of us—without benefit of lively anecdotes or fresh insights.

As the friar rambled on, my inner critic kept up a sotto voce commentary: "I've heard all this before." "Wish he'd say something new that I could chew on." "That poor man really doesn't have much to say." Ever hungry for manna yet untasted, I devalued any experience of hearing the same old thing.

After a good night's sleep, I awoke feeling as peaceful as a traveler who has at last arrived safely home. I walked across the room toward the closet. On the way I passed the sink with its small framed mirror on the wall above. Something caught my eye like an unexpected presence. I turned, saw the reflection in the mirror and said aloud, "No wonder he loves me!"

This involuntary affirmation stunned me. What or whom had I seen in the mirror? When I looked again, it was "just me," an ordinary person with a lower-than-average reservoir of self-esteem. But I knew that in the initial vision I had seen God-in-me breaking through like a sudden sunrise.

At that moment I knew what it meant to be made in the divine image. I understood right down to my size

1

eleven feet what it meant to be loved exactly as I was.
Only later did I connect this revelation with one granted
to the Trappist monk-writer Thomas Merton. As he reports
in *Conjectures of a Guilty Bystander*, while standing all
unsuspecting on a street corner one day, he was
overwhelmed by the "joy of being...a member of a race in
which God Himself became incarnate.... There is no way
of telling people that they are all walking around shining
like the sun."

As an absentminded homemaker may leave a
wedding ring on the kitchen windowsill, so I have often
mislaid this precious conviction. But I have never
forgotten that particular retreat. It persuaded me that the
Spirit rushes in where it will. Not even a boring director or
a judgmental retreatant can withstand the "violent wind"
that "fills the entire house" where we dwell in expectation
(see Acts 2:2).

So why deny ourselves any opportunity to come aside
awhile and rest on holy ground? Why not withdraw from
the daily web that keeps us muddled and wound?
Wordsworth's complaint is ours as well: "The world is too
much with us." There is no flu shot to protect us from
infection by the skepticism of the media, the greed of
commerce, the alienating influence of technology. We need
retreats as the deer needs the running stream.

An Invitation

This book and its companions in the *A Retreat With...*
series from St. Anthony Messenger Press are designed to
meet that need. They are an invitation to choose as
director some of the most powerful, appealing and wise
mentors our faith tradition has to offer.

Our directors come from many countries, historical

eras and schools of spirituality. At times they are teamed to sing in close harmony (for example, Francis de Sales, Jane de Chantal and Aelred of Rievaulx on spiritual friendship). Others are paired to kindle an illuminating fire from the friction of their differing views (such as Augustine of Hippo and Mary Magdalene on human sexuality). All have been chosen because, in their humanness and their holiness, they can help us grow in self-knowledge, discernment of God's will and maturity in the Spirit.

Inviting us into relationship with these saints and holy ones are inspired authors from today's world, women and men whose creative gifts open our windows to the Spirit's flow. As a motto for the authors of our series, we have borrowed the advice of Dom Frederick Dunne to the young Thomas Merton. Upon joining the Trappist monks, Merton wanted to sacrifice his writing activities lest they interfere with his contemplative vocation. Dom Frederick wisely advised, "Keep on writing books that make people love the spiritual life."

That is our motto. Our purpose is to foster (or strengthen) friendships between readers and retreat directors—friendships that feed the soul with wisdom, past and present. Like the scribe "trained for the kingdom of heaven," each author brings forth from his or her storeroom "what is new and what is old" (Matthew 13:52).

The Format

The pattern for each *A Retreat With...* remains the same; readers of one will be in familiar territory when they move on to the next. Each book is organized as a seven-session retreat that readers may adapt to their own schedules or to the needs of a group.

Day One begins with an anecdotal introduction called "Getting to Know Our Directors." Readers are given a telling glimpse of the guides with whom they will be sharing the retreat experience. A second section, "Placing Our Directors in Context," will enable retreatants to see the guides in their own historical, geographical, cultural and spiritual settings.

Having made the human link between seeker and guide, the authors go on to "Introducing Our Retreat Theme." This section clarifies how the guide(s) are especially suited to explore the theme and how the retreatant's spirituality can be nourished by it.

After an original "Opening Prayer" to breathe life into the day's reflection, the author, speaking with and through the mentor(s), will begin to spin out the theme. While focusing on the guide(s)' own words and experience, the author may also draw on Scripture, tradition, literature, art, music, psychology or contemporary events to illuminate the path.

Each day's session is followed by reflection questions designed to challenge, affirm and guide the reader in integrating the theme into daily life. A "Closing Prayer" brings the session full circle and provides a spark of inspiration for the reader to harbor until the next session.

Days Two through Six begin with "Coming Together in the Spirit" and follow a format similar to Day One. Day Seven weaves the entire retreat together, encourages a continuation of the mentoring relationship and concludes with "Deepening Your Acquaintance," an envoi to live the theme by God's grace, the director(s)' guidance and the retreatant's discernment. A closing section of Resources serves as a larder from which readers may draw enriching books, videos, cassettes and films.

We hope readers will experience at least one of those memorable "No wonder God loves me!" moments. And we hope that they will have "talked back" to the mentors, as good friends are wont to do.

A case in point: There was once a famous preacher who always drew a capacity crowd to the cathedral. Whenever he spoke, an eccentric old woman sat in the front pew directly beneath the pulpit. She took every opportunity to mumble complaints and contradictions— just loud enough for the preacher to catch the drift that he was not as wonderful as he was reputed to be. Others seated down front glowered at the woman and tried to shush her. But she went right on needling the preacher to her heart's content.

When the old woman died, the congregation was astounded at the depth and sincerity of the preacher's grief. Asked why he was so bereft, he responded, "Now who will help me to grow?"

All of our mentors in *A Retreat With...* are worthy guides. Yet none would seek retreatants who simply said, "Where you lead, I will follow. You're the expert." In truth, our directors provide only half the retreat's content. Readers themselves will generate the other half.

As general editor for the retreat series, I pray that readers will, by their questions, comments, doubts and decision-making, fertilize the seeds our mentors have planted.

And may the Spirit of God rush in to give the growth.

Gloria Hutchinson
Series Editor
Conversion of Saint Paul, 1995

Getting to Know Our Directors

Introducing Mary

Mary of Nazareth, Dominic de Guzman and Ignatius of Loyola will guide us in this seven-day retreat. Like Moses and Elijah conversing with Jesus on the Mount of Transfiguration, our holy mentors are not bound by the restrictions of time and space. Before entering the retreat, we pause "outside the gate" to renew our appreciation of the three wise elders who have come to enrich our experience of God in prayer.

We know Mary as the Mother of God, our Blessed Mother, Mystical Rose, Queen of Heaven. Yet to her first-century contemporaries she was simply Mary of Nazareth. She kept house, spun wool, built fires, baked bread, tended the garden, cared for her child and her husband. She watched Jesus grow from toddler to teen, from carpenter's son to the Anointed of God. How fortunate we are that she has come to teach us how to allow the Holy Spirit to pray through us in word, in silence, in stillness and in movement.

The Gospels depict Mary as a woman of deep faith whose great yes to God models the perfect response to God's call—a call addressed to each of us as well. She is a person of prayer who responded to the mystery of her Son by treasuring every sign of his divinity and pondering it in her heart. Mary is the first disciple. It is her willingness to follow Jesus and to fulfill her ministry in the Christian community (see Luke 11:27-28; Acts 1:13-14; 2:42-47) that we hope to emulate.

Throughout the ages, Mary has been contrasted to a thoroughly masculine God; she has been defined by a Church whose hierarchy is male. As Patricia Noone, S.C., notes, "The result of this one-sidedness on so many levels has been to place the burden of compensating for it directly on her: Mary stands for the feminine in Christianity."[1] This symbolic burden has engendered various imbalances in the relationship between Mary and the faithful in Church history, imbalances that the Vatican addressed when it called us to honor her "with special love" and strongly emphasized her discipleship.

American feminists present Mary as a prophetic, holy and autonomous woman. Rosemary Radford Ruether describes Mary as a "woman of the poor who belongs to a people under occupation by the great empire of her time, a refugee woman with child, an unwed mother, the mother of a son executed by an unjust state."[2] Widowed woman, survivor, sojourner, seeker of sanctuary, marginalized woman, woman pregnant with hope, Mary teaches us all how to bring Christ to a broken world.

Introducing Dominic

At Mary's side is our second mentor, Dominic de Guzman, founder of the Order of Preachers (popularly known as Dominicans). Born around 1170 in a village of Old Castile, Dominic was profoundly influenced by his mother, Juana de Aza. Before Dominic's birth, Juana dreamed of her son as a little dog who "...would issue forth holding in its jaws a flaming torch seeming to set the world on fire."[3] This image seems especially apt since Dominic, by his preaching, took the fire Jesus cast on the earth and spread it everywhere.

Dominic's childhood love of prayer and study prepared him to absorb the Scriptures as a young university student. A friend said of him:

> What he learnt with facility, thanks to his gifts, he watered with his devotion and caused to spring from it works of salvation. In this way he obtained the entry to happiness, in the judgment of Truth itself, who, in the Gospel, proclaims blessed those who hear the word and keep it.[4]

Dominic was ordained at about twenty-five; he joined the Canons Regular at Osma, where his formal ministry as a preacher began. On a journey with Bishop Diego in 1203, Dominic passed through France, where he preached against the heretical doctrine of Albigensianism which taught that matter is evil. Although the young priest had his heart set on becoming a missionary in far-off lands, Pope Innocent III charged him to continue preaching among the Albigenses. In 1216 Dominic and those volunteers who had joined him in what was known as the "Holy Preaching" were solemnly confirmed as the Order of Preachers.

Dominic established *The Little Office of the Blessed Virgin Mary* as a common prayer for the Order and ensured that the name of the Mother of God would be part of the formula for the Profession of Vows. Time and again he trusted in the Virgin's intercession as he sought unity with her Son. With our Lady's help (sometimes in miraculous ways), the Order spread rapidly. By the time of Dominic's death in 1221, the Order numbered over five hundred; sixty friaries divided into eight provinces embraced the whole of western Europe. It continued to grow through the centuries and today the Order of Preachers is known throughout the world. In 1234 Pope

Gregory IX canonized Dominic.

Introducing Ignatius

Our third mentor, baptized Inigo, was born in 1491 to the noble Loyola family of northern Spain. At sixteen, the charismatic young man went to serve as a page at the court of Castile, where he learned to appreciate the pleasures of courtly life. As the opening line of his autobiography attests, "...[H]e was a man given over to the vanities of the world, and took a special delight in the exercise of arms, with a great and vain desire of winning glory."[5] In other words, he specialized in gambling, womanizing and fighting.

The turning point in Ignatius' life came in May, 1521. Serving with the army at Pamplona, he was severely wounded by a cannonball that injured both legs. He walked with a limp for the rest of his life. His career as a soldier of Spain was over. His life as a soldier of Christ was about to begin.

Lying in bed, bored, Ignatius yearned for the romance novels of his time. There were none to be found. All that could be brought to him was a copy of the life of Christ and a book on the lives of the saints. Desperate for diversion, he began to read. As he read about the saints he began to envision a different kind of future for himself.

During his long recuperation, Ignatius wavered between thoughts of his former life of pleasure and a desire to please God. Once he had regained his strength, he went to the mountain monastery of Montserrat where he took three days to make his general confession in writing. On the eve of the Annunciation in 1522, before the statue of the Black Madonna of Montserrat, Ignatius offered our Lady his sword and dagger. He gave his clothes to a beggar and set out for Manresa, where he led a life of extreme penance, solitary prayer and ministry to the sick.

It was during this time that Ignatius, now schooled in discernment and strengthened by mystical graces, wrote *The Spiritual Exercises*. This manual for a life-changing retreat program would become his greatest gift to the Church and his most memorable contribution to spirituality.

At the age of thirty-four, Ignatius returned to school in Barcelona to prepare for university studies at Alcala. Imprisoned twice by overly zealous members of the Inquisition (who could find no error in his *Exercises*), Ignatius went on to the University of Paris, where he began to attract like-minded men, among them Peter Faber and Francis Xavier. On the feast of the Assumption in 1534, the small band of seven friends took their vows as "Companions of Jesus." Six years later Pope Paul III officially approved Ignatius' Society of Jesus. While serving as superior general, the founder sent missionaries to all parts of the world. He preached, provided spiritual direction, founded homes for the disadvantaged and carried on a voluminous correspondence.

In the early hours of July 30, 1556, at the age of sixty-five, Ignatius died in his bed at Rome. Yet the work he had established was just beginning. Already there were a thousand Companions of Jesus. Gregory XV canonized Ignatius in 1622. In 1922, Pius XI proclaimed him patron of all spiritual exercises and related works.

Placing Our Directors in Context

Our three mentors—Mary, Dominic and Ignatius—come to us from three vastly different worlds. They were all people of their times. Their experiences of God were profoundly shaped by the culture in which each one lived. Yet we know that the landscapes of culture and history change more rapidly than the interior landscapes of the heart. So despite their differences from each other and from us, we have come to a trio of wise guides who will help us navigate the pathways of the heart.

Our Lady's World

First-century Nazareth was a mere pebble in the sand compared to the great city of Jerusalem in southern Judea. In Jerusalem was the magnificent new temple built by Herod the Great, who tried to win Jewish favor by dedicating his most colossal building project to them. To this temple Mary and thousands of other faithful Jews made their annual pilgrimage of faith for Passover and other festivals. From the Jewish *Mishnah*, we learn of the nature of one such celebration—the water-drawing ceremony of the harvest festival, Sukkot: "Whoever has not witnessed the rejoicing of the festival of the water-drawing has never seen joy. Men of piety and good deeds danced with torches in their hands, singing songs of joy and praise, and the Levites made music with lyre and harp and cymbals and trumpets and countless other instruments."[6]

And yet all the Jews lived in the shadow of Rome. At festival times in the temple, hundreds of Roman guards stood perched above, lining the porticoes, ready to swoop down on any riot that might be fomenting among the passionate crowds.

Whatever Jesus' own education may have involved, his mother would not have been permitted to study the Torah or to converse with religious teachers. She would, however, have been fed by the great tradition of Hebrew

Scriptures—rich images of dancing and mourning, psalms expressing the entire spectrum of human emotion. As a devout Jew, Mary participated wholeheartedly in celebrating the great Jewish feasts, always accompanied by music and dancing, plentiful wine and meat.

She also observed the many communal rites of passage (the birth of a male child, his circumcision and presentation in the temple, his weaning and his final presentation in the temple at age thirteen). No great celebrations accompanied the key moments in a young girl's life. And yet we can imagine a deep unfolding of faith for a young and passionate Jewish girl such as Mary—wailing at a funeral in the house of a dear friend or dancing in a festive wedding procession as the bride is carried through the streets to her bridegroom's house. We can surmise that Mary, like other Jewish women, was matriarch of her household and took charge of passing along the heart of her faith to her child, telling and retelling the great stories of her ancestors.

Dominic's World

Twelve centuries after Mary, amid the political upheaval of the Middle Ages, the mendicant orders of Dominicans and Franciscans burst forth. As the population in western Europe increased and knowledge about agriculture grew, creative serfs began to find ways to free themselves from feudal lords. Liberated serfs became artisans and merchants grouped together for protection, forming towns and then cities. These citizens gradually began to divest the feudal lords of their power.

Because many of the secular clergy were propertied people caught up more with temporal affairs than with spiritual, the townspeople frequently found themselves opposing Church hierarchy in their struggle for new rights. While the bourgeois remained, for the most part, deeply religious, they were uneducated in sacred studies and looked for leaders who showed apostolic zeal, sometimes finding them among the laity. As a result, heresy gained a foothold and grew.

Two great heretical sects constantly attacked the Church, criticizing all clergy and denouncing Church authority. One of these penetrated northern Italy, where they were known as Cathari, and southern France, where they were called Albigenses. They believed that everything material or physical was evil. The other sect, known as Waldenses, was a lay movement whose members zealously embraced the apostolic life. Because the clergy refused to accept them, the Waldenses cut themselves off from the Church. Both groups contrasted their ascetic, dedicated leaders with worldly clergy; both, too, were backed by greedy magistrates who encouraged the growth of heresy in order to acquire Church possessions.

Dominic's followers responded to the need for clergy educated in the sacred sciences—excellent preachers who could also instruct the people in the faith. The Dominicans preached and taught Catholicism throughout the continent and beyond. Their way of life embraced poverty rather than property, representative assemblies instead of feudal forms of organization. Just when the pope, saddened by the unbridled growth of heresy and the deep woundedness of the Church, wondered how the situation could ever be remedied, God raised up Dominic to preach and live the word of God.

Ignatius' World

Four centuries after Dominic, during Spain's golden age, Ignatius was led by God to found the Society of Jesus.

The fifteenth century was the age of such cultural giants as El Greco, Lope de Vega and Miguel de Cervantes. It was also an age of great saints: Teresa of Avila, John of the Cross and John of God.

Ignatius was born a year before Columbus discovered America. Six years later, Vasco de Gama rounded the Cape of Good Hope, finding his way around Africa. Two years before Ignatius' conversion, Magellan began his voyage to the Pacific and Cortez began his conquest of Mexico. Three years after Ignatius arrived in Paris, Pisarro conquered Peru. When Ignatius was fifty-two, Copernicus shocked the world by proposing that the earth revolved around the sun.

Ignatius' time also saw a media revolution. For the first time books began to be available to the average person. Small tracts could be used to convert, reconvert or lure people away from the faith. At least twenty new universities were founded in Spain in the sixteenth century. Ignatius and his men would make a significant contribution to the education of youth, founding forty-six colleges in Europe before the saint's death.

Doctrinal dispute was rending Western Christianity. Ignatius was Martin Luther's junior and John Calvin's elder. Luther nailed his ninety-five theses on the cathedral door at Wittenburg, Germany, in 1517—just four years before Ignatius was wounded at Pamplona. Luther was excommunicated at the Diet of Worms in the same year Ignatius was converted in the midst of his convalescence.

In England, Henry VIII broke with Rome in 1531, seizing the monasteries' land and wealth and pronouncing himself free to marry Anne Boleyn. Three years later Ignatius and his first companions gathered in Paris to pronounce their first vows and put themselves at the disposal of the Roman pontiff, Paul III. A year later Thomas More was beheaded in London. The Society of

Jesus was founded in 1540, a year before Calvin published his declaration of beliefs in his *Institutes*. The Council of Trent opened in 1545.

Notes

[1] Patricia Noone, S.C., *Mary for Today* (Chicago: Thomas More Press, 1977), p. 109.

[2] Rosemary Radford Ruether, "Mary's Role in U.S. Catholic Culture," *National Catholic Reporter*, Vol. 31, No. 15, February 10, 1995, p. 17.

[3] M. H. Vicaire, *St. Dominic and His Times*, trans. Kathleen Pond (London: Darton, Longman and Todd, Ltd., 1964), p. 21.

[4] Ibid., p. 27.

[5] *St. Ignatius' Own Story, As Told to Luis Gonzalez de Camara*, trans. William J. Young, S.J. (Chicago: Loyola University, 1980), p. 27.

[6] *Jewish Liturgy, Prayer and Synagogue Services through the Ages*, ed. Raphael Posner, Uri Kapluon and Shalom Cohen (New York: Leon Amiel, 1975), p. 55.

DAY ONE
Opening Our Hands

Introducing Our Retreat Theme

We have it on the word of God: Our bodies are temples of the Holy Spirit (see 2 Corinthians 6:16). Our Lady, Dominic and Ignatius have much to teach us about how we worship in these temples. For those who picture Dominic and Ignatius as intellectuals with a cerebral approach to God, our retreat theme may come as a surprise. Both these male saints were practical, passionate, emotional individuals who answered Christ's call in concrete, vivid ways. Both men were powerfully affected by their relationship with Mary. In our retreat, we will explore the passionate loving which characterized our mentors' prayer lives. And, in the process, we will reclaim the wealth of gesture and movement from our Jewish and Christian traditions.

This retreat focuses on physical ways of worshiping the incarnate Son of God, Jesus. It is a plan for spiritual exercise and an opportunity for spiritual delight. Simply reading the plan, like reading an exercise manual, is not enough. We have to actually *pray* the meditations to gain the benefit. We must allow ourselves time to savor the taste of each day's prayer as one would enjoy a box of rich chocolates. Our Lady, Dominic and Ignatius invite us now to exercise with them our capacity for whole-hearted prayer and to delight in Christ's greater glory.

Opening Prayer

O Mary, your heart was virgin soil, open for the
planting.
By the power of the Spirit,
the holy seed took root in your humble garden
and you bore the fruit of a new creation.

As your yes to God rings through the centuries,
help me open my heart to the Holy One.
Help me open my hands in prayer.
Help me have the courage to say yes to God's call.

O Dominic, passionate preacher, chaste lover,
courageous truth-bearer,
I come to ask you about living the Word of God,
letting go of all that is not God,
lighting the way with truth and joy.
Walk closely with me through these seven days
so that I may burn with the fire of faith
and the flame of hope and enter, as you already have,
the heart ablaze with love,
the very heart of God.

O Ignatius, loyal companion to our Lord,
Teach me that new beginnings are always possible.
Pray that I may believe that our God
makes all things work to the good of those who love.
Teach me to believe that God is my truest friend,
my most loyal companion.
Pray that I in my flesh may live always
and do all things always for the greater glory of God.

Amen!

RETREAT SESSION ONE

Focus your imagination for a moment upon the heart of Jesus. Imagine you are able to move into this vast expanse, a home so immense that all who choose love find welcome there. Here in the heart of our God is perfect peace. Here dwell in blessed harmony all those who have been proven faithful. In confident faith, let us call out the names of our three guides for this retreat:

"Mary!" "Dominic!" "Ignatius!"

Trust in the power of this prayer. Trust beyond what your senses tell you. Trust in this holy communion of saints. First you see only three glimmers of light. But gradually the light takes shape and you recognize our trusted saints.

First you see our Lady, beautiful beyond description! Dressed in a simple tunic edged in gold, her dark hair covered lightly with a veil, she is indeed full of grace. She stands before us as a young teenager, now as a pregnant virgin, now as a woman in full bloom, now as a grieving widow, now as a woman clothed with the sun. Her appearance radiates her fullness.

Two men approach us. One is dressed in black and limps slightly. The other wears white with a cord tied round his waist. Both carry rosaries. Both are tonsured— one by nature; the other by choice. One holds a little book; the other a walking staff.

Light streams from all three faces. There is peace here, and wisdom for the asking. We come to our mentors to learn about the mystery of opening to God's presence. Too often we have imagined God as distant. Today we seek to worship a God who is far closer than we could ask or imagine. We pray for the grace to remove the self-made obstacles that blind us to this presence. We pray to be opened by the gift of the Holy Spirit: opened in our hearts, our souls, our bodies, our minds, our whole selves.

Mary speaks first.

Mary: Welcome! We have come at your bidding to share with you the treasures of our hearts, a share in the treasure of his Sacred Heart.

Dominic: Yes, welcome, friends. I rejoice in your choice to be with us with Jesus.

Ignatius: Fellow pilgrims, your culture is far busier than ours were. Our Lady, Dominic and I lived in times when it was easier to slow down. The times in which you live make this a harder choice. But you are here. You have chosen wisely. Welcome!

Mary: Our retreatants have come to unburden their hearts. Shall we not share with them some of the secrets of ours?

Dominic: Dear Mother, then you should begin. You are our Lady and our Queen.

Ignatius: Well spoken, sainted friend.

Mary: When my story begins, I am a scant thirteen years old. Thirteen! In those years when the blush of puberty sat newly on my cheeks, I struggled with the new forces rising in my body. I dreamed of my husband-to-be, Joseph, and wondered what it would be like to marry him, to lie with him. My body burst into womanhood, and my girlfriends and I shared our secret thoughts about marrying and bearing children and becoming mothers and lighting the lamps at Shabbat.

Yet even as we whispered and wondered, I found myself too shy to share my deeper thoughts. Inside were my prayers—my questions, my inner longings to know my place in the world, to know God's will for me and to be a truly holy woman, like Sarah and Miriam of old. So I found myself taking these prayers to God. While I was hanging the laundry, sometimes the blue of the sky would overwhelm me, the wind whip round my ankles and billow out the bedclothes like the sails of ships. How could I help but breathe deep the Spirit of the wind, breathing all the way down to my belly? Sometimes I would burst into song. You see, the boys went to the synagogues to pray and study, but I just let the psalms well up in me like the ones we used in our processions on feast days. Oh those processions! Blasts of the trumpet, lyre and harp, clashing cymbals, drums and dancing! So I would gather up my laundry basket and process out to the fields singing:

> O come, let us sing to the LORD;
> let us make a joyful noise to the rock of our salvation![1]

Dominic: Oh, yes, Mother, I too felt those deep stirrings in my soul. When I walked from city to city I spent long hours out in nature. I came to understand this as a kind of traveling prayer. The kiss of the sunlight or the tickle of the rain, the laughter of the wind and the song of the brook: Oh, how they spoke to me of God.

Ignatius: The tickle of the rain? Dominic, you are much more a poet than I. But I confirm what you're saying of the power of God's creation to awaken us to wonder. I used to lie on my back for hours just gazing at the clouds.

Mary: Yes, beloved sons, each of us has felt that wonder and joy surging within us, just as the psalmist did:

> Praise God in his sanctuary;
> praise him in his mighty firmament....
> Praise him with tambourine and dance;
> praise him with strings and pipe![2]

Ignatius: What God taught me at Manresa, Mother, was that we are created by God, for God—to give God praise and thanks. When we do this, we discover who we are and why God placed us on earth.

Dominic: You make it sound so simple and logical.

Mary: It is simple, but not easy. Never easy! Even in the days of my youth, I was old enough to know of the turmoil in the streets, the struggle of our people under an alien rule. My people, like the Israelites of old, longed to be set free—free to live the Torah with our whole lives, not fearful from moment to moment of our fate in the hands of the Romans. I longed to dance as Miriam did at the crossing of the Red Sea—exuberantly!—and as David danced, whirling before Yahweh with joy. If only our people, too, could know the taste of freedom. But what could I do?

So, I prayed. I prayed for courage. Miriam had the courage to get her brother Moses plucked safely from the bed of the river and trained in Pharaoh's own palace to lead his people to freedom. David, a mere shepherd boy, had the courage to defy the most terrifying of the Philistines. And so I spoke to God:

> To you, O LORD, I lift up my soul.
> O my God, in you I trust....
> Make me to know your ways, O LORD;

teach me your paths.[3]

Oh, the innocence of my trusting! My heart goes out to
your teenagers today, struggling to know their own
identities, to make an impact on the world. How do they
pray? And who will help them to pray?

I know the violence that lurks in your streets, the
discontent, the longing which no drug can dissipate. How
do *you* pray? The great God has a purpose for you, just as
for me. Are you willing to open your hands and offer
yourself to God's plan?

There in the rhythm of my young woman's days, I
opened my hands to God. And suddenly, I heard a sound
like the wind, and I was enveloped in light. A voice spoke
to me from out of the brilliance and bade me rejoice,
calling me highly favored, declaring the Lord was with
me! I was deeply disturbed by these words. Perhaps
someone had been watching me as I prayed in the field,
perhaps I was too bold, perhaps.... But the voice went on,
assuring me I had found God's favor and calling me to
bear a son. Not just any son: My son would be king! My
son would be Son of *God*!

My heart leaped in my chest as I tried to understand. I
was confused. I wasn't even married yet. How in the
world...? I couldn't help it; I just blurted it out: How can
this be since I am (I whispered) a virgin? The Holy Spirit
would come upon me, cover me like the cloud on Mount
Sinai when Moses received the covenant.... Could I really
say yes to this?

But it was time to answer. My hands were trembling.
They closed with fear near my chest. The angel told me
not to fear, but how could I not? I wanted to say, "But I am
too young! Surely there is some other girl more confident,
more holy...." But suddenly something awakened inside of
me. It was ancient and it was new and I could not hold

myself back. "Here am I, the servant of the Lord; let it be with me according to your word."[4]

My whole life was made new. My hands were still trembling, but they were open—just as my eyes were open, just as my heart was open to that greater will. I was open, open to grace, open to miracles, open to God.

Dear friends, are you willing to open? Let me show you the way. Pray with me.

Mary's Open Hands Meditation

When you pray, open your hands. Open your hands now. I know this may feel awkward at first. Praying with your hands closed or clasped may feel safer! When you open your hands, you are leaving yourself vulnerable, and you never know quite where God is going to lead you.

Imagine the angel of God standing before you, looking at you lovingly, light streaming toward you. When the angel calls you by name, stand in greeting. If your heart trembles, close your hands into your chest and take a moment to acknowledge your doubt, your fear. Remember, courage doesn't mean feeling no fear; it means being willing to risk, to act, to move even when you are afraid.

Your fear may be the nudge of the Spirit calling you beyond anything you've ever known. So go ahead and prepare yourself by closing up tight. A flower closes up at night, all petals folded in, preparing itself to burst open at morning light. Ready? Take a deep breath. Open. Open your eyes. Lift up your heart. Let the light of the Lord stream into your whole being, body and soul. Let the angel bear God's message of love to you, even as I heard it some two thousand years ago. Let that love wash away all worry. Worthy or unworthy, you stand in the light of the Lord. God has chosen you in your own unique way to be a Christ-

bearer. May you, too, say yes to the call!

Dominic: My friends, freedom in the Spirit sounds so liberating that we all long to live in it. We do not have to fight to obtain it, for Jesus has invited us to live as sons and daughters of God, as children of light. We only have to let go of the darkness and open ourselves to the light and to freedom, as our Mother Mary did!

Ignatius: Brother Dominic, when I heard what you endured for the sake of the gospel, my heart was set ablaze. Please tell these pilgrims something of your life. Let them learn of the freedom of which you speak.

Dominic: I went to Rome, where the pope commissioned me to preach the truth. Although I had no carefully charted plan, I knew Jesus had sent preachers before me and had told them:

> Go on your way. See, I am sending you out like lambs into the midst of wolves. Carry no purse, no bag, no sandals....[5]

How simple; how freeing! I was on my way. I had one simple tunic and walked barefoot.

Yes, my dear friends, hunger and cold and weariness traveled with me. Sometimes brutal enemies of the truth wanted to kill me; there were hungry wolves and swollen rivers along the way. But I didn't have to guard my riches or hold onto a certain reputation. I didn't have to worry about who liked me and who hated me. Jesus had promised to journey with me, and I knew I was safe with him.

Jesus has promised to journey with you, too, good friends. Go with him. Trust him. Spend time with him—

especially in the stillness of the night.

To pray throughout the night was a special gift I received; not many understood it. One night my companions and I arrived at our halting place chilled to the bone. I was eager for some time alone with my Beloved. A church stood nearby, and I hurried there for the warmth I was seeking. I lost myself in Jesus.

During those times of prayer, I positioned myself in ways that helped me come closest to my Beloved: I stood before the crucified Christ, arms outstretched like his, holding nothing, just open to receive love. Sometimes I opened my arms gradually, asking Jesus to take from me the heaviest baggage—worry about the mission, worry about my brothers and sisters, worry about the fate of sinners. As Jesus lifted my worries from me, I found my arms stretching ever wider until I stood in the form of a cross. And there, in this strange open-armed embrace I found freedom, rest, joy and strength.

Trust Jesus, dear friend. Go before him now with whatever heaviness your heart carries. And now I will share with you a brief meditation that comes from my experience.

Dominic's Cross Meditation

Hold both arms out straight in front of you, hands open, in a gesture of pleading. Next, name one worry that weighs you down and pray, "Jesus, I entrust this to you."

Trust him. Open your arms a little. Name something else you can hand over to Jesus and pray, "Jesus, I entrust this to you."

Continue in this way, opening your arms a little more each time until they are stretched in the form of a cross. Let Love embrace you as you focus on Jesus crucified.

Ignatius: I must be honest and say, Brother Dominic, that the Spirit rarely taught me to pray that way! Now it's not that I'd get embarrassed or anything like that, but my gestures were more traditional and straightforward. The movement in prayer that I spoke of was the interior movement of the Spirit.

Dominic: And that's all part of God's plan. As you yourself discovered in giving the *Spiritual Exercises*, each of us is different, a true original.

Ignatius: Yes. Exactly. I was always amazed that no two people responded in exactly the same way. There are, to be sure, rules and guidelines, but the Holy Spirit moves in each of us in a unique and beautiful way.

Mary: You keep using that word *exercise*. Tell our friends why that analogy is so apt.

Ignatius: Well, just as our bodies need exercise, so do our souls. Let's begin by acknowledging that we have a lot of flabby Christians around.

Fellow pilgrims, we need to crawl before we can walk, to walk before we can run. So let's proceed slowly, at a snail's pace, and know that the Lord is right with us, as he was with the disciples on the road to Emmaus.[6]

Don't think that you need to do everything Dominic or I or our Lady did. Trust the Spirit to guide you. Remember, "it is not so much knowledge that fills and satisfies the soul, but the intimate understanding and relish of the truth."[7] Don't be like a tourist rushing through the art museum, trying to take it all in instead of finding a few great works and spending time with them. Try different postures in prayer: standing, kneeling, lying down and so forth. But when you find a posture that helps you and brings delight to your soul, don't go changing to another position just to change.[8]

Often we think of prayer as simply lifting up our hearts and minds to God. This is a good start, but it doesn't go far enough. We are not angels. To be a human being is to be a spirit wedded to flesh. Therefore we need to know Christ in and through our flesh. God is within us, around us and among us. Our task is to heighten that awareness, and pray that our love will be translated into acts of love.

One of the ways that the Lord taught me to pray was to meditate on one word or phrase of a vocal prayer such as the Our Father.[9] As you try this, concentrate on your breathing. All living things breathe: plants, animals, humans. To stop breathing is to die. How powerful it is to become aware of this simple rhythm of life—taking in breath and releasing it.

Your culture understands better than mine did the scientific principles at work here. I knew nothing of oxygen intake or carbon dioxide. But perhaps my culture understood the significance of this action better. I did know that by the breath of the word of God the heavens were made,[10] that Adam came to life at the breath of God,[11] that Jesus breathed the Holy Spirit into the disciples.[12]

Let your prayer be as simple as your breathing. I'm going to suggest a series of one-minute prayer breaks, mini-spiritual exercises, having to do with breathing.

Four One-Minute Spiritual Exercises

1) *Breathe in through your nose and exhale through your mouth. Take the breath all the way into your belly. Don't try to puff up your chest like some old soldier. Breathe slowly and deeply, as if you were relishing the taste of each*

and every breath.

Ready? Take one minute right now simply to focus on your breathing, taking in breath and letting it go—the most basic rhythm of life.

How was that? Relaxing? But not as easy to do as it sounds, is it? For most folks the hard part is quieting their minds. Our thoughts fly by so quickly in all directions.

2) *Let's add another element to make the prayer connection a bit more explicit. The Lord taught me to pray with my imagination. We use our imaginations all the time, sometimes productively, often destructively. Imagination plants seeds in our souls.*

Imagine that your breath is the very presence of the Holy Spirit. Remember that the Hebrew word for "breath" is ruah, *the same word that is used for the Spirit, the holy breath of God.*

Take in the presence of God with each inhalation. As you exhale, let go of all that is not of God. Pray for one minute with this focus. If other thoughts crowd in, simply notice them and then release them with the exhalation. You may find it helpful to close your eyes. Now take another one-minute prayer break to heighten your awareness of God's loving Spirit.

3) *Now let me suggest another element that may make it a bit easier. When the disciples asked Jesus to teach them to pray, he taught them the prayer we call his: the Lord's Prayer. It begins with the words "Our Father." The Hebrew word is* Abba; *perhaps "Our Daddy" is a better translation.*

With each inhalation, pray "Our Father" or "Our Daddy" or simply "Daddy" slowly and attentively. Let the sound resonate within you, like the long, beautiful echo of a well-made bell. Try this now for one minute.

4) *Finally, try this: As you breathe in, pray "Our Father" or*

"Daddy"; as you exhale pray the word "Jesus." For Jesus is the living Word of God.

This is a beautiful prayer to the Trinity. Imagine that the Holy Spirit is truly coming inside you, connecting you to the Father and the Son. Try it now for just one minute.

This kind of prayer is powerful medicine. And yet most people can practice it only for short periods of time, because it requires such concentrated focus. Practice it just a few minutes a day. And it will help build your prayer muscles for other more involved kinds of meditations.

I believe in taking advantage of all the resources God gives to us. While you're praying this kind of exercise, close your eyes or focus your eyes on a picture of Jesus. When you inhale, think of taking in the presence of Jesus through your eyes. As you exhale, imagine yourself reaching out and touching Jesus through your breath, through your eyes, through your hands, through your heart. You may find soft music helps to round out the prayer. Music can be like a river that carries you along.

Fellow pilgrims, use your senses to support your prayer.[13] They can lead you to God or away from God. Culture uses the senses to continually lead you into temptation by what you look at, what you eat, what you hear, what you speak. Our senses are not bad. Our Creator made them to help us find our way back to God. When Jesus told us that it was better to lose one eye than to go to hell with two eyes,[14] he wasn't recommending mutilation. He was telling us to use all for the glory of God, misusing nothing of what God has given. What we need to cultivate, companions, is an openness to the presence of God. The Lord is near, but we need to train our awareness in vigilant faith, enduring hope and constant charity to recognize the presence of our hidden God.

For Reflection

- As I begin this retreat, I ask our great God to help me name some of the heavy things that I hold onto, forgetting that God is reaching out to lift them from me.

- Do I sometimes find myself trying to placate God as if God were a mean, vindictive person rather than the God of peace? Or can I really be with God as God is— unconditionally loving and perfectly able to accept how I really feel and think? I ask God to help me give voice to how you feel about divine love in my life.

Closing Prayer

The Sign of the Cross[15]

To conclude this day of retreat, we meditate on the Sign of the Cross.

In the name of the Father,

Begin by planting your feet firmly on the ground. Stand with your hands hanging loosely at your side, your knees gently relaxed. Breathe deeply of the Lord's love. Take in all the strength and goodness that you need. With each exhalation, let go of all the worries and cares of this day.

Place your right hand in the center of your forehead as we pray, "In the name of the Father." Pray in the name of our loving Creator, who loves us more tenderly, compassionately, completely than any earthly mother or father could.

Gently massage the center of your forehead. In the traditions of yoga, this is the third eye, the center of creativity. For many of us, this is simply the center point of a headache.

Pray that we may surrender all the functions of our mind, our memory, our intellect, our will, our imagination, into the loving care of our Creator God, whom Jesus called Abba. Continue to breathe deeply.

And of the Son...

Now lower your hand to the center of your chest, as we pray "in the name of the Son." We pray in the name of the wounded Sacred Heart that the wounds of our own hearts may be channels of peace. We pray in the name before all other names, before whom every knee in the heavens, and on earth and under the earth must bend: We pray in the name of Jesus. Continue to breathe deeply.

We pray that our hearts of stone may become hearts of flesh. We pray that the frozen parts of our hearts may melt before the fire of love that burns in the holy heart of Christ. Continue to drink deeply of this love.

And of the Holy...

Place your hand on your left shoulder as we pray in the name of the "Holy." Claim your past: the deeds you are proud of, the deeds you are ashamed of. Hold on to what is to be held. Let go of all that is to be loosed. God makes all things work to the good. Nothing that we've done, nothing that has been done cannot be transformed into a channel of blessing, a pathway to peace by God at work in our lives. Continue to breathe deeply.

Spirit.

Now lift your hand and place it on your right shoulder. Surrender your future to the power of the Spirit. Acknowledge that whether we live a long life or a short one, in sickness or in health, in riches or in poverty, in honor or disgrace, we will never be orphaned. God will not abandon us. God's Spirit will abide.

Now bring your hands together in holy unity, palms together, fingers pointing beyond this earth, feet firmly planted in the realities of life.

Amen.
Amen to the God beyond us, the God of power and wonder, mystery and surprise, more immense than the universe, more vast than the sky.

Amen to the God who lives among us, who creates community, who reconciles our differences, who calls us to be Church.

Amen to the God who dwells within us, in the heart cave, in the secrecy of our self.

It is in the name of this God, the one God— Abba/Daddy, Son/Jesus, holy Holy Spirit—that we sign ourselves this day.

Notes

1 Psalm 95:1.

2 Psalm 150:1b, 4.

3 Psalm 25:1-2a, 4.

4 Luke 1:38.

5 Luke 10:3-4.

6 See Luke 24:13-35.

7 *The Spiritual Exercises of St. Ignatius,* trans. Louis J. Puhl, S.J. (Chicago: Loyola University Press, 1951), #2, p. 2.

8 See *The Spiritual Exercises,* #76, p. 36.

9 See *The Spiritual Exercises,* #252-256, pp. 110-111.

10 See Psalm 33:6.

11 See Genesis 2:7.

12 See John 20:22.

13 See *The Spiritual Exercises,* #121-125, pp. 54-55.

14 See Matthew 5:29.

15 This is based on a meditation that first appeared in *The Body at*

Prayer: Guided Meditations Using Gesture, Posture and Breath.
Meditations by J. Michael Sparough, S.J., and Bobby Fisher
(Cincinnati: St. Anthony Messenger Press, 1987).

Day Two
Reaching in Trust

Coming Together in the Spirit

Once there lived a man named Frank, who prayed his trust in God's love for him would grow. One day the circus came to town. To drum up publicity for the event, a tightrope walker staged a public demonstration of his skill, advertising that he would walk a tightrope stretched across the ravine at the edge of town.

Curious to see if it could be done, Frank showed up to watch. The wire swayed precariously in the breeze. The performer eyed the crowd and asked if they believed he could walk across the ravine. Neither Frank nor anyone in the crowd thought he could do it.

Effortlessly, the performer crossed the wire and returned. A second time he addressed the crowd, asking them if they believed he could push a wheelbarrow full of potatoes across the wire. This time the crowd was divided, some cheering "Yes!" and others jeering "No!" Once again the performer crossed the wire and returned, potatoes and all, with apparent ease. Frank led the applause, cheering louder than anyone else.

Finally, the performer addressed the crowd, asking them if they believed he could take a person in the wheelbarrow across the wire. This time Frank, along with everyone else in the crowd cheered with one voice "Yes."

There was not a doubter in the crowd. "So," said the tightrope walker, "you all believe that I can do it? Now who will prove their belief and get into the wheelbarrow?" The crowd grew suddenly silent, and Frank regretted praying that the Lord would increase his trust.[1]

Defining Our Thematic Context

The poet W. H. Auden named our time "the age of anxiety." From the time of Adam and Eve we have learned to distrust God, living in shame and guilt about our own shortcomings. In our first session, Mother Mary, Dominic and Ignatius invited us to pray to be open to God's presence in the world and in our lives. They each suggested a simple exercise or meditation to facilitate this process. In this session they challenge us to courageously trust in God's love for us. They remind us that we are created to give God praise and glory. We celebrate our lives and our bodies as gifts from God and pray to use them for God's greater glory.

Opening Prayer

Trust[2]

Dear Dominic, Beloved Ignatius, Blessed Mother
    Mary,
in your presence, I admit the truth hidden in my heart.
I've read books on trust. I've heard tapes on trust.
I've written journals on trust. I've preached sermons
    on trust.
But let's begin by admitting: I don't trust you, God.

I'd like to trust you. I've prayed to trust you.
I've told others to trust you. I've told others I trust
   you.
But the truth is closer to fear. I'm afraid. I'm afraid of
   you.
Yes, you: all-judging, all-seeing, all-knowing you.
Yes, me: semi-controlled, semi-consistent, semi-
   confused me.
I'm afraid of what will happen if I ever really entrust
   my life
to your all-powerful, almighty, all-just and all-
   hopefully merciful hands.
I've heard stories about your sainted friends,
waiting dark nights in the cells of their souls,
losing their heads at the most inopportune times,
fed to the lions for lunch,
or dressed up for dinner, roasted medium rare.
You see I've talked to your son, and he assures me
no servant is greater than the One who sends.
So, yes, I trust you'll lead me to a lonely hill
where three nails and two wooden cross beams are
   waiting.
This won't come as a welcome surprise.
And to tell you the truth I can't trust you'll return
three days later to keep your promise to roll that stone
   away.
I've been abandoned and betrayed already, thank you.

The most I can muster is to entrust to you my heart—
five minutes at a time.
Come, take me as your own.
I give you all I am, and all I ever hope to be.
I am your servant, your friend, your child.
Transform me, possess me, liberate me, fill me.
Do with me what you will—five minutes at a time.
Then, please, come back again.

Knocking at the door of my heart,
Re-extend the invitation.

RETREAT SESSION TWO

Mary: Today I want to tell you about my own journey in trust. For trust, like a rose, unfolds its petals slowly. I remember those first few days of pregnancy. I carried the seed of new life—the miracle child—within me, but no one knew! I bore the most amazing of all secrets deep within my heart, gently unfolding in my womb. My whole being welled up with a song of God's marvelous goodness:

> My soul magnifies the Lord,
> and my spirit rejoices in God my Savior,
> for he has looked with favor on the lowliness of his
> servant.[3]

Ignatius: It took me much longer to be able to believe God actually wanted me. I had to be shot by a cannon!

Mary: I must admit I prefer the visit of an angel to a cannonball!

Ignatius: Had I been less stubborn, God would have had an easier time getting my attention. Many times I had to read, "[Y]ou are precious in my sight, and honored, and I love you..."[4] before I could actually believe it was meant for me.

Dominic: Scores of people tried to convince me that

matter is evil. But how could we be evil if the Son of God was born of you, Mary, flesh like our flesh? And yet it took me many years to pray with the psalmists, "I praise you, for I am fearfully and wonderfully made."[5]

Mary: I know well your prayers to crack open the hard shell around your hearts. Many a night I poured out my love for you. I wanted you to be on fire with love. I wanted you to know the God who loves us with more tenderness and strength than any earthly mother or father.

This is the love I knew in the depths of my soul. This is the God to whom I said "yes." And I wanted you—I want every person—to be so filled with the Spirit that you would shout for joy and dance through the night! But I know from my own experience that it was one thing to receive a divine message in prayer, but quite another thing to let that message dance through your whole life in a radically new way.

The transformation was a gradual process for me as well. The song of praise bubbled up in me, but the world was not ready to let the song be sung. Nor was I. After all, I would have been stoned for being unwed and with child! And how could I tell Joseph? Would *anyone* believe me? With whom could I share my soul?

Perhaps this is why my heart has always gone out to the little ones, like Juan Diego of Mexico. I gave him a vision of hope for his people, ravaged by disease, invasion and slavery, and he made me known to the world as Our Lady of Guadalupe. I have always reached out to those who fear for their safety, like the mothers of the disappeared in Latin America, the Muslim women brutalized in Bosnia. I stand firm to protect the children, and I hold in my heart the old ones who dream dreams and the young ones who see visions.[6] I choose the simple ones, just as God chose me, to bring hope to a broken world. I am guardian of the poor, the outcast, those who cry out for comfort and compassion. I am their mother.

Ignatius: I know you as mother. So often I prayed to you when I needed help. And yet somehow it is hard for me to imagine that there was a day when *you* needed help.

Mary: Yes, mother to all I have become. But in those moments after conception I was only mother-to-be. Old reality had fallen away, and the new had not yet come to pass. I knew what it was like to carry the ecstasy, the urgency of a divine message, but not how to bring that to birth in the world. When Paul spoke about it, he said,

> We know that the whole creation has been groaning in labor pains until now; and not only the creation, but we ourselves, who have the first fruits of the Spirit, groan inwardly while we wait for adoption, the redemption of our bodies.[7]

Ignatius: When I was wounded I, too, groaned! Not just from my shattered leg, but because I could not bear the truth of my own sins. It was like looking into a cruel mirror. How could God want me?

Mary: Ah, yes, but listen to Paul as he continues:

> ...the Spirit helps us in our weakness; for we do not know how to pray as we ought, but that very Spirit intercedes with sighs too deep for words. And God, who searches the heart, knows what is the mind of the Spirit, because the Spirit intercedes for the saints according to the will of God.[8]

So God came to me in my weakness. I had no words, but suddenly I knew where I needed to go—to my cousin Elizabeth. She, too, carried a miracle. Perhaps she would accept my story and help me still my heart. To the arms of my sister in spirit I fled. As I walked, I imagined growing fuller with this child, giving birth to him and nestling the small one to my breast. But then the fear once again gripped my heart. I imagined an angry voice shouting at me, calling me vile names. I took refuge in prayer.

When I arrived at Elizabeth's house, anxiety tightened my throat. But I forced myself to call her name, "Elizabeth!"

Her greeting flooded my ears: "Blessed are you among women, and blessed is the fruit of your womb."[9] She knew my mystery; she called me blessed! I fell into her wise arms. My tears welled up and I wept. Elizabeth was an angel to me, a sister, a safe haven for my soul. And she, too, carried a miracle child. At the sound of my voice, her baby leaped! I touched her belly, so round and full, and I felt her baby kicking, stretching, reaching out to greet this child of mine.

We talked and laughed, the old and the young learning from one another, leaning into each other's ways. I held her well-worn hand in mine. How many loaves of bread had she baked in her long years? How many yards of cloth had she spun and woven? I saw the wrinkles round her eyes and the creases in her brow. "Elizabeth," I asked her, "are you afraid?"

"Mary, God planted these children in our wombs. Now God will give us all the strength we need to bring them to birth, love them and let them go to their destiny." Then Elizabeth took my hands and looked into my eyes. "...[B]lessed is she who believed that there would be a fulfillment of what was spoken to her by the Lord."[10]

O, my Lord, I do believe! In Elizabeth's arms, I was overwhelmed with joy. I felt like Hannah when God blessed her with a son, and finally my song of praise found its full voice and poured out of my being, no holding back. I invite you to join me in my prayer.

Mary's Magnificat[11]

My soul magnifies the Lord
(and I danced, for I had become the new Ark of the Covenant);

Holy is your name
(I lifted my arms)!

Your mercy reaches from age to age for those who fear you
(and I reached first to the right, then to the left, embracing the wide, wide Kingdom of God).

You have shown the power of your arm
(I sent my arm forward with all my might, leading the nations);

You have scattered the proud of heart
(I turned and flung my arms apart).

You have pulled down princes from their thrones
(I reached above me and pulled down all who abused high places),

and exalted the lowly
(and from the earth, I lifted the little ones up to the arms of God).

The hungry you have filled with good things
(I gathered all God's goodness into my lap),

the rich sent empty away
(and I waved away all who hoard).

You have come to the help of Israel, your servant
(I lifted my arms overhead, then drew God's blessing to my heart),

mindful of your mercy
(I opened my hands once again)—

according to the promise you made to our ancestors—of
your mercy to Abraham and Sarah and their descendants
forever

> *(I passed my hand in a long swoop from left to right, seeing*
> *before me all the faces of all my ancestors whom God has*
> *loved and all the descendants ever to come).*

Amen!

> *(After I danced, Elizabeth took me in her arms and we*
> *rocked. O, the Spirit moving in our midst, turning our lives*
> *upside down! The revolution within us, between us, rocking*
> *the world around us!)*

Ignatius: How often I have meditated on the story you just told. And it continues to invite me to reflect on my own story, of the graciousness of God's love.

Dominic: Amen, Ignatius. Dear retreatants, take time, as we did, to reflect on how God is at work in your lives.

Ignatius: That reminds me of when Francis Xavier and I were studying together at the University of Paris. The Lord had already pulled me by the hair of my head—

Dominic: Oh, you had hair in those days?

Ignatius: Yes, the Dominicans of the Inquisition left me with one or two.

Mary: Brothers, brothers! No wonder your followers had such a hard time getting along with each other.

Dominic: Oh, Mother, you know a jest is food for the soul. I want our friends here to feel right at home. We walked the earth with flesh and blood just as they do now. We were not created as angels or pure spirits. We were far from perfect.

Ignatius: He's right, my Lady. Too many of our companions look at us as nothing more than plaster statues. You knew fear, Mother, and confusion and sadness. So did we. But through it all God was teaching us to trust.

Mary: You are right, my sons. Beloved retreatants, receive the wisdom of their storytelling.

Dominic: I never tire of hearing the tale of you and Xavier.

Ignatius: Xavier and I were studying at the University of Paris. He had looks, money, brains and charm. Every woman within fifty miles of Paris was interested. But there was within Francis a hunger that all the popularity in the world could not satisfy. I could see it in his eyes when he came back to the dormitory after too much wine. I could feel it in his heart when melancholy settled upon him.

Therefore I beat on his heart with the persistence of a drummer. "Francis, what does it profit you if you gain the whole world, but lose your soul?"[12] Once, twice, a hundred times I hounded him like the persistent widow knocking on the judge's door, begging for a settlement.[13] Finally, we struck a deal. Xavier agreed to make the *Spiritual Exercises.*

Dominic: And he was never the same after that.

Ignatius: Like a master baker, the Lord prepared in Francis' heart the bread of salvation.

Mary: Yes, my sons, the Lord our God wants us all to be converted from our sin and selfishness and brought into the joy of his Kingdom. But it is work to change; it takes time to reflect on our lives and discover what God's plans are for us. Remember what was written through Jeremiah the prophet: "For surely I know the plans I have for you, says the LORD, plans for your welfare and not for harm, to give you a future with hope."[14]

Dominic: Tell them how you first learned this truth, Ignatius.

Ignatius: After I was wounded at Pamplona, I was a broken man on the mend. God had me where God wanted me and used my sickness to bring me closer. I thought a successful career as a soldier a sign of God's favor. My health, appearance and social connections all seemed to be such signs. And yet I abused these gifts to simply advance my own social standing, to fan the flames of my own lust and to fill my longing for power, control and domination of others.

I now look back and see that shattering my leg was one of the greatest gifts God ever gave me. Had I been left to my own devices, I might well have continued a life of uninterrupted sin. That which I feared most became the source of rich blessing!

Mary: And I thank God for the suffering that Joseph and I endured because it taught me greater trust and dependence on God in all things.

Ignatius: I formulated this idea in what I called *The Principle and Foundation of the Spiritual Exercises.* We are created for God. When we give ourselves to God and not to false gods, we discover our happiness. Everything else is God's gift to help us achieve that happiness.

Mary: So many things we think will bring us happiness make us miserable.

Ignatius: And some things that we think will make us miserable end up teaching us valuable lessons. Our task in life is to learn to discern which choices will lead us to God and which will lead us away.

Dominic: Did reading my story and that of Saint Francis lead you to a wise choice?

Ignatius: When I read the life of Francis of Assisi and your life, Dominic, something deep inside me stirred. I knew I was reading the truth. I was challenged with a new vision of what life was all about. I thought to myself, "If Dominic and Francis could do great things for Christ, then why can't I do the same and even greater?"[15]

I was imprudent. I was naive. There was a lot of pride in the challenge, but my heart was breaking open to a whole new meaning of love. Step by step, lesson by lesson, the Lord was teaching me as a master tutors a young pupil.

But, of course, it wasn't easy. Even the brightest fire produces ashes. I became bored with all those pious reflections. My fervor began to fade. To amuse myself, I began thinking about the pleasures of my previous life.

I excelled in womanizing, gambling and dueling. No one ever threw so much as a disparaging glance my way without feeling the tip of my sword. I carried sharpened steel in my hand and on my tongue. I knew not the meaning of the term purity. But I did know desire and revenge, anger and power, prestige and domination and the intense pleasure these emotions can give. In my bed of convalescence, I burned the sheets with the flames of my imagination. But when the flames burned out, I tasted ashes.

I turned again to the saints, and they in turn led me to Christ. I felt my heart burning within me. I had never known such pure joy, holy love. I was changing—no, I was being changed. I felt a strange, new wonderful presence, a power coming through me, but not of me. I was being transformed from the inside out. I was what Jeremiah described: clay on the wheel.[16]

Dominic: And did you choose Christ from that point on in your life?

Ignatius: I wish I could say that I did, but I wavered. I grew restless, agitated, angry. When the boredom returned it was almost intolerable. I grew irritable with the servants. My family brought me no comfort. I retreated to the world of my imagination to drink in sin-soaked pleasure—but once the goblet was dry, my pain was increased, not diminished.

And yet when I drank from the chalice of Christ, the aftertaste was sweet. One day, as you say, the light went on, and I saw the very different results these thought patterns were producing. Both brought me pleasure, but of different sorts. One left me agitated and thirsting for more without any satisfaction. The other brought me pleasure and left me with peace.

Mary: And at that moment you began to learn to say yes to God and no to the evil one!

Dominic: Learning to discern what is from God and what is from the evil one requires a holy balance. One of the great abuses of this present age is the abuse of the body.

Yet it is one of the greatest gifts God has given us. We only have one body and we are to protect and to care for it well. We don't know what it means to be human except in and through our bodies.

Mary: Throughout human history there have always been heresies that reject the beauty of the human body by viewing sexuality with fear and suspicion. There was a strain of this excess in the Essenes at Qumran.

Ignatius: As there was in the Manicheans of Saint Augustine's time, in the Illuminati of my age and in the Jansenists of seventeenth-century France. This error has been handed down into your own age, fellow pilgrims.

Dominic: That was the major heresy that I fought throughout my life.

Ignatius: You're referring to the Albigensians, no doubt.

Dominic: Because Pope Innocent III recognized the destructive force of the Albigensian heresy and kindred false doctrines, he charged my friend Bishop Diego and me to go out to preach the truth among the heretics.

Let me explain. The Albigensians believed in two gods, a good one whose Son was Christ and an evil one whose son was Satan. Matter, they held, was essentially evil. The greatest of all sins was sexual intercourse, even in marriage; sinful also was possessing material goods, eating flesh and many other things. So great was their abhorrence of matter that some even thought it an act of religion to commit suicide by voluntary starvation or to starve children to death.

I tried to explain that our bodies, our minds and our spirits were all created good by a loving God, the only

God. You will understand this situation, dear friend, because I see shades of this heresy in your own day.

Dominic: How many, because of an overrated work ethic, pour out their lives in order to accumulate goods that can't last? How many starve their children—if not from food, from time spent with them?

Mary: How many people, feeling their bodies inadequate in a culture that overvalues thinness and beauty and devalues acceptance of all people as they are, fall into such sicknesses as anorexia nervosa, bulimia or chronic overeating?

Ignatius: How many try to kill anxieties and/or boredom with alcohol and other drugs?

Mary: How many have lost respect for the sick, the aged and the unborn? How many reports of murders, rapes and other crimes cover the pages of your newspapers every day? How many kill another person's reputation to look good or to get ahead?

Dominic: How far we have strayed from God, who loves us as we are made—body, mind and spirit! Are we falling into a heresy of separation—what I believe in my mind is good; what I do with my body doesn't matter?

Dear retreatants, let God's love shape you into persons prepared to live forever! Remember what our Mother Mary told us earlier in this reflection. After she said yes to God, her whole being surged with new life. I found that when I said yes to preaching the truth, I was pregnant with such hope and joy that I could not keep from sharing it with others. Yes, I was discouraged. Yes, I was afraid. But I thank God that I never lost my hope. O friend, Jesus wants to be born in you. Feel his life surging through you, even as your heart aches. Break bread with another and discover that the power of Jesus' love can fill the most dismal of human circumstances.

Such a life needs nurturing—exercise, healthful food, discipline, gentleness, rest. Let us enter into this wholeheartedly—body and spirit. Take good care of yourselves, for you have been chosen to give birth to the Christ in your own time.

Ignatius: This was a difficult lesson for me to learn. In the early days of my conversion I was far too hard on my body. I put lye in my food to destroy the taste. The result was that I ruined my stomach and suffered from ulcers for the rest of my life.

Dominic: How hard it is to learn a holy balance—neither to pamper our flesh nor to abhor it. Remember, dear friends, how important it is to allow your individuality and your own situation in life to shine forth in your prayer. For example, some of the brethren wrote after my death about my "Nine Ways of Prayer." I'm sure my prayer took more than nine expressions, but these might help you to find your own forms of praying.

Dominic's Nine Ways of Prayer

1) *Praying while traveling. I often walked from place to place in an effort to preach the word. You may drive more frequently than walk, but it doesn't matter. What better time to praise God than when you are surrounded by so many of your brothers and sisters on a crowded expressway!*

2) *Studying God's word. Of course, I loved the word of*

God. Studying Scripture is certainly an act of prayer because it draws us into communion with the living God.

3) **Genuflecting before the cross.** It is by Jesus' cross that we can all come into the Kingdom, so genuflecting often before an image of our crucified King expresses devotion.

4) **Doing bodily penance.** Penance is truly an expression of prayer, for it helps us to keep a holy balance with our bodies, minds and spirits.

5) **Praying in the form of a cross.** Sometimes it helps to model our own bodies in the shape of a cross so that we remember that it is by sharing in Christ's suffering that we are brought to his glory, that it is our sins he endured.

6) **Bowing before the altar.** The altar is a sacred place. Through the Masses offered there daily, Jesus' sacrifice is made present to us. How good to bow low in the presence of the living God at the altar!

7) **Praying while prostrate on the ground.** Sometimes I would be so overwhelmed by a sense of sin in and around me that I would need to prostrate myself before the Lord and beg his mercy.[17]

8) **Arching heavenward while praying.** At other times, I would so long to be united with God forever that I would stretch my body heavenward.

9) **Praying with hand and arm gestures.** I cannot relate all the many ways I used my hands and other bodily gestures to express my inward prayer, but you will do the same once you find your body in tune with your spirit.

These are the "Nine Ways," friends, but I invite you to explore and express your praises, petitions, thanksgiving and contrition in your own ways.

Ignatius: I always admired the freedom with which you prayed, Dominic.

Dominic: Many people may ask, "Does it make any difference if you pray standing or kneeling or sitting? How should we hold our hands and arms in prayer? Is it better to pray with open eyes or closed eyes, head raised or head bowed?" Athletes, dancers and lovers know well that our bodies express more than the conscious mind intends to express.

Ignatius: I've always believed that each person has to discover the particular way the Spirit desires to lead him or her to the mystery of God, who is beyond all our words and ways and methods. You [may be] familiar with what I wrote to Francis Borgia in 1548:

> [T]hat level [of prayer] is best for each particular individual where God our Lord communicates himself more.... He sees, he knows, what is best [for each one] and, as he knows all, he shows [each one] the road to take. What we can do to find that way with his divine grace is to seek and test [the way forward] in many different fashions, so that an individual goes ahead by that way which [for him or her] is the clearest and happiest and most blessed in this life.[18]

Dominic: I suggest you guide our retreatants through a series of different prayer positions. This will help them understand how body posture can affect both the form and the content of your prayer.

Ignatius: This I will happily do, but I remind our fellow pilgrims that the goal in all our prayer is to find God. Everything else is a means. "People are held back on the road to finding God when they (or those who are helping them) become so preoccupied with the means or so attached to a particular way that they lose clarity about the end."[19] Hold what I say lightly because God is always larger than our methods.

Fellow pilgrims, before we begin, make sure you have enough room to stand up straight and raise your arms over your head, to stretch your arms out to your side and to lie flat on the ground. Perhaps a little soft instrumental music will help guide you and relax you. A favorite statue, crucifix or holy picture may also help to focus your gaze.

Ignatius' Prayer Experiment in Body Posture[20]

Begin by sitting in a comfortable chair, preferably without arms. Below are variations of four hand and arm postures: hands open, hands cupped, hands crossed and palms together. Take a few minutes to pray in each of these four positions.

As you pray I invite you into a state of relaxed alertness. Hear the voice of the All-Holy in your heartbeat; imagine God present in your breathing. Picture yourself praying before Jesus himself.

As you pray, remember to breathe in life and grace and strength. Exhale all that blocks the Lord's grace in your life. Pray the prayer of your heart, the prayer that you alone can pray—with or without words.

1. Hands open

2. Hands cupped

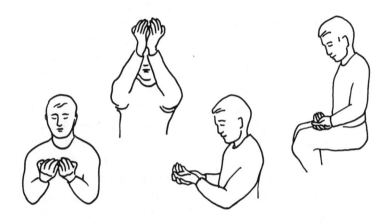

3. Hands crossed

4. Palms together

I suggest that after you have prayed in each of these postures that you go back to one or two that felt most comfortable for you. Try praying with your eyes closed, and then experiment by opening your eyes and focusing on a holy picture or statue. Note which is your preference.

At a leisurely pace experiment with different prayer postures: lying down, sitting or standing while breathing deeply and offering the prayer of your heart.

Now bend your back into a simple or a deep bow. Keep your knees unlocked. Bend your arms at your elbows and let your palms face the sky. With bowed back, pray the prayer of your heart.

Turn now to that posture in which you found it the easiest to pray, the most challenging or reassuring. Pray in that position the prayer that you alone can pray. Pray with your heart, with your mind, with your body as the Spirit dictates.

Dominic: Well led, Ignatius! Fellow pilgrims, in addition to these ideas, I believe Christians of your age could learn much from studying yoga, Zen meditation and some of the prayer disciplines of the non-Christian religions of the East. Yet I agree with Pope John Paul II when he writes that "first one should know one's own spiritual heritage well and consider whether it is right to set it aside lightly."[21] There are dangers: Many Christians of your day know neither the rich and diverse Catholic Christian tradition nor anything more than a smattering of the prayer practices of other world religions.

Ignatius: We want to avoid mere external worship, for that can lead to sheer hypocrisy.[22] But most Christians in the 1990's are not suffering from too much attention to external detail in their prayer. Far from it!

Dominic: Why is it that we can be so creative when it comes to striking a business deal or delighting guests, but when it comes to preparing for the Lord's coming into our hearts, we're all thumbs?

Mary: This is an awareness that needs to be cultivated. Our hearts naturally yearn for God, but that yearning can be hidden by sin and laziness.

Ignatius: You can also understimulate your senses so as to evoke a holy hunger for God. For example, you might go on a silent retreat for a weekend or try driving your car without turning the radio on or switch your phone off for the evening. Pay attention to what your body is telling you, and it will help lead you to God's door.

Mary: Thank you, Ignatius; these are all helpful suggestions for using the gift of our bodies for prayer. I, too, have a few suggestions for our retreatants. It's a meditation on hands that you must pray with someone else, a sister or brother, spouse or fellow sojourner on the road. When you pray with another, you can touch and bless each other as Elizabeth and I did. And may you know Christ in your midst.

Mary's Meditation on Hands

Focus on your own breath. Let the rhythm of your breathing become calm and deep, reaching deep into the well that is you. As you breathe into your belly, give breath to the Christ within you.

Now, look at your hands. What do you see? Look at your skin, as it stretches around the contours of bone and sinew and vein. Notice all the little lines criss-crossing, circling, drawing across your palms. Are your hands old or young? Are they feeble or strong, calloused, nimble or knotty? Do you wear any rings that tell about your life and the commitment of your heart? These hands, once so tiny and tender, how have they grown? Who has washed your hands, held your hands, hoped for your touch?

What is the work of your hands? How many dishes have you dried, nails have you driven, documents have you drawn up? What bread have you baked, bills have you paid, pictures have you painted? How many gardens have you grown, fists have you pounded, tears have you wiped away? What birth and death have you held in your hands, what wounds have you tended, with what tenderness have you touched? What wounds have you inflicted? What fingers have you pointed in blame? What doors have you slammed shut?

Now open your hands. For this moment, hold your life in your hands: all the receiving and rejection, all the work for justice, all the loving and longing and letting go. Blessed be the life in these hands.

If there is any particular area of your life that needs a special grace now, hold this need in your hands. Beyond that, you don't need to do anything—only receive.

Now gently take your partner's left hand into yours and cradle it lightly between your two palms. The left side of the body is associated with receiving, so holding your partner's hand with loving reverence, pray silently for your partner's need. After a moment, if you feel comfortable, you can take your partner's palm and touch it gently to your cheek and pray that your partner's need may be met with tenderness. When you are finished say, "Blessed be these hands that need."

Replace your partner's left hand, and take the right hand between your two palms. The right hand is associated with giving, so this time pray silently for all your partner's *unique gifts, the time and talents your partner offers to the world. Bless the life that you hold in your hands.*

Before letting go of your partner's hand, touch your partner's palm to his or her cheek, praying that God may do great things in and through this person. When you are finished, pray, "Blessed be these hands that give." Before letting go, take both hands in yours and pray the words "Blessed be these hands." Let your partner respond, "Amen."

Switch roles so that each of you both gives and receives blessing. Notice if one role is more comfortable to you than the other. Some find the act of giving easier than receiving, because receiving often puts us in touch with our vulnerability. Whatever your experience, let God speak to you and touch you with tenderness. Blessed be your hands! Amen.

My prayer for you, dear friends, is that these prayer exercises will help you to grow in trust each day of the retreat. When we begin to open in trust to grace, we are God's fragrant blooms.

For Reflection

- How do I show that I trust God to provide for my happiness?

- In what ways can I affirm myself and others as fully loved by God?

- God created me human—neither body nor spirit but both, a whole. In what specific ways do I deny the goodness of my body or my spirit?

Closing Prayer

The Hail Mary

Mary models for women and men alike the fullness of human trust. As Mary said yes to the movement of the Spirit in her life, we now do likewise.

Opening Stance

Begin standing in a traditional posture of prayer: palms together, fingers pointing up. For a moment, close your eyes and imagine Mary, the queen of wholeness and holiness, standing before you. See Mary opening her hands and opening her heart to receive your prayer.

'Hail Mary...'

In a gesture of reverence to this holy woman of God, bow your head and pray: "Hail Mary. O Mother, we greet you, we welcome you into our midst." Then come upright once again.

'Full of grace...'

With your palms up, cross your hands at your wrists. In a sweeping motion, uncross them and spread them out gently in front of you and pray: "Mary, model of openness, you teach us how to say yes to God's invitation. We stand with you, our sister, and open ourselves to God's grace."

'The Lord is with you...'

In another sweeping motion, scoop both hands a little to your right, then up high to the God of heaven. Now, draw that great God to your heart, crossing your hands over the center of your chest. "Mary, the God of compassion dwells in your heart; help us know this God in our hearts."

(Starting position)   Hail Mary,   full   of grace,

the Lord   is with you.   Blessed are you among women,   and blessed is the fruit of your womb,   Jesus. (to left)

Holy Mary, Mother of God   pray for us sinners   now   and at the hour of our death.   Amen.

'Blessed are you among women...'

As we echo Elizabeth's words, gently move your palms to face Mary, fingers pointing up, blessing her. "Mary, we honor you as woman pregnant with hope; teach us to carry hope in our hearts."

'and blessed is the fruit of your womb...'

Lower your hands to your belly over your own womb, real or imagined. "Mary, you carried the Christ child in your body, allowing God's creation to come to fruition through you. Help us to know our bodies as holy. May our lives, too, bear the fruit of Jesus."

'Jesus...'

Now turn your hands to your left as if you were cradling the Christ child. "Mary, as you cared for Jesus, so are we called to care for all children of the earth. Font of compassion, teach us to see Christ in all God's children. Make us refuge for the homeless, defenders of the oppressed."

'Holy Mary, Mother of God...'

Bring your hands out to your sides, and lift them up, making a large circle that meets at the top. "Mother of all, we are your children. Enfold us in your all-encompassing embrace."

'Pray for us sinners...'

Once again, bring your palms together and lower your hands down to the front of your chest. "Teach us to fear God less and trust God more."

'Now...'

Cross your hands over your heart. "Mary, Mother of Mercy, pray for us; hold us close to your heart. For now is the only time that God's grace can touch us—not in the future, not in the past, but here in this present moment."

'And at the hour of our death...'
Lower your hands to your sides, palms facing forward.
"Mary, source of consolation and healing, as you held your son in death, hold us. Carry us into the Kingdom, now and forever."

'Amen.'
Bow your head. "So be it. Amen."

Notes

1 The original source of this story is unknown. This retelling is original to the authors.

2 This poem first appeared in *Presence*, Vol. 1, Number 1, January, 1995.

3 Luke 1:46-48.

4 Isaiah 43:4.

5 Psalm 139:14.

6 See Joel 3:1.

7 Romans 8:22-23.

8 Romans 8:26-27.

9 Luke 1:42b.

10 Luke 1:45.

11 Based on Luke 1:46-55.

12 See Mark 8:36.

13 See Luke 18:1-5.

14 Jeremiah 29:11.

15 *St. Ignatius' Own Story*, p. 9.

16 See Jeremiah 18:1-7.

17 Unknown to Dominic is an interesting parallel: In Japanese culture, bowing is an expression of honor. The more profound the bow, the greater the sign of respect. To prostrate oneself before another is the greatest expression of giving honor back to a person whom one has offended.

18 *Letters of St. Ignatius of Loyola*, trans. William J. Young (Chicago: Loyola University Press, 1959), p. 181.

19 Ibid., p. 3.

[20] This prayer exercise is based on an audiotaped meditation in *The Body at Prayer: Guided Meditations Using Gesture, Posture and Breath*. Meditations by J. Michael Sparough, S.J., and Bobby Fisher. Cincinnati, Ohio: St. Anthony Messenger Press, 1987.

[21] *Crossing the Threshold of Hope* by His Holiness John Paul II (New York: Alfred A. Knopf, 1994), p. 90. The pope recommends that people who are interested in studying the prayer and meditation practices of other world religions first read the brief document *On Certain Aspects of Christian Meditation* (October 15, 1989) by the Congregation for the Doctrine of the Faith.

[22] See Matthew 23:5.

DAY THREE
Cleansing Our Hearts

Coming Together in the Spirit

In a short story called "Somebody's Son," Richard Pindell describes the plight of a runaway boy. The opening scene shows the boy writing a letter home to his mother, confiding how he hopes against hope that his stubborn father might forgive his waywardness and accept him back. The boy describes his plan: "In a few days I'll be passing our property. If Dad will take me back, ask him to tie a white cloth on the apple tree in the field next to our house."

Days later, we see the boy seated on a train, moments from his house. The tree will appear as they round the next bend. But the boy can't bear to look out the window. What if there is no white cloth? Desperate, he turns to the man next to him, and says, trembling, "Mister, will you do me a favor? Around the bend on the right, you'll see a tree. See if there's a white cloth tied to it."

The train rolls by the tree. The man answers with amazement, "Why, son, there's a white cloth tied to practically every branch!"[1]

Defining Our Thematic Context

With the help of Mary, Dominic and Ignatius we have meditated on the gift of our bodies and the gifts of creation. We have prayed for the grace to trust in God's plan for each of us, which is always for our well-being.

Today we look at the shadow side of our existence. We acknowledge that we, like Adam and Eve, have not lived fully in God's love. Our mentors call us to honest self-assessment and to cleansing our hearts in God's merciful love. They teach us to grieve for the sin of the world and to call upon the healing power of forgiveness.

Opening Prayer

Mary, Dominic, Ignatius,
I beseech you, lend me your hearts.
Mine is burnt and indelicately smudged.
And my hands—do not hold them.
These palms are covered with soot,
clinging to the smoldered leaves
of last year's triumphs;
ashes, ashes, we all fall down.
My heart is gone;
numb, zipped up, ripped out.

Now only emptiness fills the space.
And since this desert needs water
I cannot help but shower it
with yesterday's fears,
crowding my eyes with tears.
I have been tempted, you know,
and have failed to resist the self-deceit
of bread and power and applauding angels.
So I am left alone in this desert,

receiving no just desserts
because there is nothing to deserve.
I wander in a whirl of feelings,
trying to take control of the shifting sands,
but constantly losing my balance.

Jesus, full of the Spirit, was led by the spirit
into the desert for forty days.
My Lord and my God,
you spoke away the devil—
but me? He seduced me.
This desert is not you deserting me,
it is me deserting you.
This dark night is not the absence of you
(you are easy to believe in);
it is the absence of me
in the irresistable arms.
Can it be that the loss of me
can clear courses in the sand to you?
Lord of the dance, lead me through this desert.
Perhaps you are leading me even now.
Am I so audacious
as to think I can thwart you?
In my weakness is your strength.
Search for me.
When you find me,
bring me home.

RETREAT SESSION THREE

Ignatius: Dear friends, remember when the prodigal son
finally came to his senses after squandering all his father's

money? And he gathered the courage to go home to his father and say, "Father, I have sinned against heaven and before you."[2] What a courageous moment of honesty and humility! We are all called to such honesty, owning our own weaknesses and taking responsibility for the pain we have caused in the lives around us.

Mary: How true, Ignatius. And yet what I see so often is that my children are afraid to be so honest. They run far from God's arms. They cling to every kind of false security, keeping themselves looking good in the eyes of their neighbors, their families, their entire world.

Dominic: Your culture, fellow pilgrims, is uncomfortable with the concept of sin. But we cannot grow toward spiritual maturity unless we confront the ways in which our sin has harmed ourselves and others. We cannot find our way back to God's arms without first admitting that we are lost.

Ignatius: And the process of humbling oneself is not easy, is it, Dominic? For so many years I hid behind the armor of my false self. So I know we are all tempted to turn away from parts of ourselves that we don't want to acknowledge. One modern Jesuit, William Barry, points out that the state of sin is characterized by the unwillingness to see oneself as a sinner.[3]

Dominic: Yes, Ignatius. And when we deny our sinfulness, we feed Satan, the father of lies.

Ignatius: That's what happened in the Genesis story. Not only did Adam and Eve eat of the fruit of the forbidden tree, but also when God questioned them, they refused to own their sin. Instead, Adam blamed Eve and Eve blamed the serpent.

Mary: And the result was that Adam and Eve knew shame. Their nakedness no longer felt like a thing of beauty and innocence. They hid themselves away, covering over their guilt, bracing against their vulnerability.

Dominic: We all play that game. How hard it is to take responsibility for our actions and to say, "I did this. I knew it was wrong, but I did it anyway. Forgive me."

Ignatius: To be able to see our sin is a great grace! So I urge you, my fellow pilgrims, to pray for this grace. To pray about sin is not to fear being judged by God, but to acknowledge who we are and what we have done, to let God love even the parts of ourselves we are afraid to love.

Mary: Ignatius, will you lead our friends in prayerful meditation?

Ignatius: Holy Mother, I would be honored to do so. I have found that sometimes a physical gesture can help our deepest selves express what our conscious minds shy away from.

Ignatius' Water Blessing[4]

Place a small bowl of holy water on a table. If possible, add a vigil candle in a small bowl that will float on top of the water. This juxtaposition of fire and water is a wonderful symbol for the holy balance for which we strive in the spiritual life.

If you do not have water that has been previously

blessed, then begin by stretching your hands over the water and praying that God's Holy Spirit will bless this gift to make it a holy instrument of grace for your life.

Now pray for the grace to know your sin and then bless those parts of your body that symbolize where you are blocked in your relationship with God. Mark them with a simple sign of the cross, and ask God to bring his light and love to these humble parts of yourself.

For example, if you know yourself to be closed-minded, dip your fingers into the holy water and mark your forehead with a cross of blessing. If there is nothing wrong with your hearing, but the members of your family or the people at work claim that you don't listen to them, then bless your ears that you may hear.

Perhaps you have eyes that do not see, even though you don't need glasses. Or perhaps your eyes are looking for love in all the wrong places. Bless those eyes. If your eyes shoot daggers and flash fire, douse the flames and sheath the daggers with a holy blessing.

Perhaps your tongue is a rudder steering you toward a shipwreck. Or perhaps your tongue is a lighted match, and you find yourself daily barbecuing loved ones, pray for a change of menu with a holy blessing of your mouth and tongue.

If the words get stuck in your throat, and you do not speak the truth because of fear, shame, cowardice or intimidation, bless your throat.

If your neck has turned to leather, and you find yourself to be a descendent of the stiff-necked ancestors who defied the Lord with their quarreling and wrangling, pray to soften it with God's grace.

If you've lost heart because of grief, or if you find that your heart of flesh has turned to stone, gently strike the rock but once with the rod of truth and love.

If you find that your God is your belly and you are

70

living for what you taste, touch, eat, drink, smoke, or snort, or if you fear how you look because of what you eat, pray the Spirit of healing to come with this blessing.

Perhaps your sexual organs have led you into infidelity, or you have sought out sexual pleasure without spiritual integrity. Bless your sexuality. Pray that you may know your body as a temple of the Holy Spirit and glorify God with it.

Perhaps you've gotten lazy. Then pray for the energy to get up and find the strength to do God's work. Bless your holy rump!

Perhaps your hands are clutched in fear or clenched in resentment. Perhaps they have grown greedy and grasping for the treasures of this world. Bless these hands.

Maybe you are stuck, not going anywhere, even though your life may be filled with lots of meaningless activity. Bless your feet. Bless them that you may have the strength to go where you need to go and to do what you need to do.

My friends, reverence your body. Honor the wounds of your life and the struggles of your life. Bless yourself often with holy water. Wash yourself often in the living waters of God's Word.

And once you have blessed yourself, bless others: Bless your spouse. Bless your children and invite them to bless you. Bless your parents, living or deceased. Bless those whom you love. Bless those whom you do not love and who do not love you. In this way we prove that we are God's children. What a holy habit this is!

My friends, I suggest you carry a small bottle of holy water with you or store one at home or at the office. Then you can bless yourself or others whenever you are in need. Prayers like this can take as little as two minutes and can be very powerful in relieving stress and refocusing us on the truths of our faith. Let these short prayers be like the sounding of a chime. One doesn't always need an hour of *meditation in the middle of the day. Even a pint of gas can keep a car from running dry.*

Dominic: Ignatius, thank you for this guidance in blessing. How did you come upon such a powerful way of praying?

Ignatius: Well, I must admit that the experience of praying for and accepting God's blessing has not always been easy for me. For that reason, one of my favorite Scripture texts is the story of Jacob.[5] Do you remember it, my friends? Jacob is visited one evening by a mysterious stranger. Eventually they are drawn into a wrestling match that lasts all night. Jacob cannot defeat the stranger, but the stranger either cannot or will not best Jacob. After an all-night battle, the stranger touches Jacob near the sciatic nerve by the hip socket. Jacob writhes in pain but manages to demand a blessing of this creature, whom he recognizes as an angel.

The angel blesses him and gives him the name *Israel*, "one who has wrestled with God." Our life with God is a holy wrestling match. Too often we think that it should be simple and painless if we manage to stay free from sin. But our God is a jealous—or should I say "zealous"?— God who wants all our hearts. The process of surrendering to this God can sometimes seem like a wrestling match. God is willing to fight with our stubborn selves to win us over!

I've always felt a kinship with Jacob because of my battle wound. Even though my knee healed, it did not heal perfectly. I walked with a limp for the rest of my life. Like Jacob, I had a life-changing encounter with the angel of God, who wounded me and blessed me. My heart was changed as a result of that meeting. My limp was a constant reminder of the man I used to be, and the new man I was called to become.

Dominic: Limping on earth that you might dance in heaven!

Ignatius: Precisely!

Dominic: One of our best dancers, I'd say.

Mary: Dear, dear sons, what's a mother to do with you?

Dominic: O holy Mother, help us continue to pray. We laugh now, but the subject of sin is no laughing matter.

Mary: How true, Dominic. Many of my children deny sin. Taking the first step of naming and owning it is important. But some get caught here. Often I see these children paralyzed by shame, hardened by guilt and caught in the trap of self-hatred. For these, the weakness lies in being unable to claim their own beauty and goodness in God's eyes. They have rejected themselves at the core of their being, most often because they have never known the gift of unconditional love. When my children do not know love at their very core, they find all sorts of twisted ways to reach out for love or attention. How ardently I pray for those who do not know how to allow God's healing love to release them from the damage of sin!

Dominic: Yes, Mary, I know many children who are wounded by physical, psychological or sexual abuse at a very young age. The scars of abuse and other wounds can be buried deep inside the human heart to fester; unexpressed rage can become masked as "wounded will."[6] For this reason, we must never presume to judge another's actions. Only God can look into a person's heart and mind and know how free that person was at the time of an action. Each of us must learn to take responsibility for our own healing.

Mary: It is extremely difficult to escape deep emotional scars. And yet God is always reaching out to embrace the hurting ones with healing love. God's love can transform even the deepest wound.

Ignatius: That is why I find myself praying often for the gift of courage. I pray that all God's children may have the courage to heal, to be made whole in God's love. For I am deeply concerned that when we block out that healing power, we open ourselves to destructive forces. And this is just the opening Satan looks for! The evil one sizes us up and attacks us at our weakest point.

Dominic: What do you mean by the "evil one," Ignatius?

Ignatius: I see the force of evil at work in three different places. First is the darkness of our own hearts when we hold ourselves away from love. Through weakness, we can fall away from serving in love and instead, serve the false god of sin. This means we choose our own narrow, fearful way over God's great healing path.

Second, there is sin in those around us. This includes the collective sin of society. We are often blind to this all-pervasive reality, but we need to recognize the pain in the world around us and make changes that allow God's light to bring healing.

Third, there are evil spirits: Satan and his fallen angels. This is not a popular notion within your culture; but remember that God's love is always more powerful than the negative energy of those spirits who wish to lure us away from righteousness and bring disruption to our lives.

Mary: That reminds me of the story in Revelation about the woman clothed with the sun crying aloud in the pangs of childbirth.[7] There at her feet was a huge red dragon ready to devour her child. How striking an image this is of my experience in bringing my son to birth! How strongly I had to cling to God, trusting in the divine plan even in the midst of the evil forces that roam the world!

Dominic: Thank God for you, Mary. Until you came along, there were a lot of people who looked at the story about Eve and began to think women were the cause of evil. Talk about putting the blame on someone else's shoulders!

Mary: You're right, Dominic. And yet to counteract this image of woman as the evil temptress, some people have tended to put me too high on a pedestal. They have tended to emphasize my physical virginity as the root of my purity. My obedience to God was the bedrock of my holiness. Some people forget that I was human, too. To understand properly the special role I have been given is to glorify God's goodness.

Ignatius: The Church has called you the second Eve. You faced the seductions of sin that we all face, and yet you chose to remain faithful to God's love.

Mary: God provided me with singular graces but, like Eve, I had to choose. Many times it would have been easier to give in to pettiness, superficial piety or self-protection. And yet God gave me the grace to continue to choose the challenging path of love, even when others around me closed their hearts. For example, some of the most outwardly religious people of my time began to place far too much emphasis on externals. I always taught my son to go deeper. And as you know, Jesus caused a lot of uproar among them by honoring the spirit of the law over its letter.

Dominic: Yes, we've heard a few of those stories: Jesus dining with sinners and healing on the sabbath.

Mary: Jesus stood up to the hypocrisy of some religious leaders of our age. His anger blazed against their self-righteousness. He had no patience for those who stood in arrogance:

> Woe to you, scribes and Pharisees, hypocrites! For you tithe mint, dill, and cummin, and have neglected the weightier matters of the law: justice and mercy and faith. It is these you ought to have practiced without neglecting the others. You blind guides! You strain out a gnat but swallow a camel![8]

Ignatius: Many religious people have a hard time integrating Jesus' anger with their view of Jesus' mercy.

Mary: My son is always kind and compassionate to the repentant sinner. But the arrogant and the proud my son confronts with their own blindness.

Dominic: So we must pray for the gift of repentant hearts, so that our eyes may be opened.

Mary: Dominic, will you lead our retreatants in a prayer of repentance? Let us ask God to open our eyes and cleanse our hearts.

Dominic: Certainly, Holy Mother. Dear pilgrim friends, when sadness because of sin (your own or that of another) overwhelms you and you realize that only God's life, which we call grace, can save, you may find comfort in praying Psalm 51. This is the same psalm that David prayed in remorse for his sin with Bathsheba. I invite you to pray this psalm with me by embodying the words through movement. I offer some of my favorite postures, but feel free to explore others that you find personally appropriate.

Dominic's Meditation on Psalm 51[9]

Lie prostrate on the floor.

> Have mercy on me, O God,
>   according to your steadfast love;
> according to your abundant mercy
>   blot out my transgressions.
> Wash me thoroughly from my iniquity,
>   and cleanse me from my sin.

Kneel with your head bowed and cross your arms over your chest.

> For I know my transgressions,
>   and my sin is ever before me.
> Against you, you alone, have I sinned,
>   and done what is evil in your sight,
> so that you are justified in your sentence
>   and blameless when you pass judgment.
> Indeed, I was born guilty,
>   a sinner when my mother conceived me.
>
> You desire truth in the inward being;
>   therefore teach me wisdom in my secret heart.

Rise and stand with your arms at your side and your back slightly rounded.

> Purge me with hyssop, and I shall be clean;
>> wash me, and I shall be whiter than snow.
> Let me hear joy and gladness;
>> let the bones that you have crushed rejoice.
> Hide your face from my sins,
>> and blot out all my iniquities.

Stand straight with your head raised to heaven. Cross your arms over your heart.

> Then I will teach transgressors your ways,
>> and sinners will return to you.
> Deliver me from bloodshed, O God,
>> O God of my salvation,
> and my tongue will sing aloud of your deliverance.

> O Lord, open my lips,
>> and my mouth will declare your praise.

Stand upright and gradually open your arms toward the heavens.

> Create in me a clean heart, O God,
>> and put a new and right spirit within me.
> Do not cast me away from your presence,
>> and do not take your holy spirit from me.
> Restore to me the joy of your salvation,
>> and sustain in me a willing spirit.

Mary: Thank you, Dominic. There is so much joy in reconciling with God. Remember, my children, when you set your foot on the road toward Yahweh, God runs out to greet you, overjoyed to welcome you home.

 Now we are ready to take the next step in our journey.

Ignatius: I know where you are leading us, Mary. We must confront the terrible face of sin that exists outside ourselves. When there is sin in our own hearts, at least we can do as the Hebrew word for "reconciliation" describes: We can turn our hearts around and come home to God's loving arms. And yet when we confront the evil that exists outside ourselves, we often feel powerless.

Dominic: My dear retreatants, do you see the sin in the world around you? Do you feel the pain? The alcoholic mother and father bicker incessantly; their children suffer the consequences. One grows to adulthood denying the need for commitment and intimacy; another's repressed anger breaks into violence; a third lives in constant anxiety, trying to please everyone and, failing, gives way to despair.

A greedy factory owner decides to dump toxic wastes into a nearby river. A dishonest politician accepts a bribe to skip safety checks on an office building. A worker wanting to get ahead makes a coworker appear incompetent by carefully placed pieces of gossip. Employees steal and cheat, making insurance burdens weigh more heavily on all. A reckless driver speeds to his own destruction and also kills a family of four. Murder, rape, hunger, sickness, ignorance: God has not created these horrors. We have.

Mary: Yes, Dominic. How do we respond to such pain? I remember that sometimes at night I would sit and weep by Jesus' bed when he was a child. I could not hold back my tears. O, the pain of our world! And the pain of your world. Even though my son came to bring new life to all generations, the pain of life remains still, two thousand years after his death. The Herods still roam the earth, the innocents are slaughtered still in many war-torn nations

and the dragons of more secret abuses prowl the world.
What about the young girl molested by her father or the
young boy by his parish priest? What about the women
beaten by their husbands, the migrant farm workers
exploited and the laborers laid off by corporate
millionaires? What about parents with Alzheimer's
rejected by their children and homosexual sons, HIV
positive, rejected by their parents?

In the days of our ancestors, a plague, a famine or an
attack by enemies called for a festival of lamentation. Our
people congregated and a fast was proclaimed. We tore
our clothes, the men shaved their heads and, like Job, we
covered ourselves with dust and ashes. The priests led our
people to the temple and there we cried out with moaning
and prayers for forgiveness.[10]

I know that the women of Bethlehem must have
gathered like this and mourned together the loss of their
infant sons at the hands of Herod. As Joseph and I made
our way into Egypt, how I longed to join in their dances of
lamentation. How I longed to pour out my grief in the
company of all my mourning sisters, like the pilgrims who
go to the Wailing Wall today, the western wall of the same
temple where I myself once prayed. There the Jewish
people join in a powerful prayer called *davening*. They
chant ancient prayers and rock back and forth in grief. I
longed to pray with such heartfelt depth. So, I carried my
grief with me until I was safe. Then, like the women in
funeral processions who wail loudly over a death, I
allowed myself to cry.

> O Lord, God of my salvation,
>   when, at night, I cry out in your presence,
>   let my prayer come before you;
>   incline your ear to my cry.[11]

Sometimes Joseph would come and be with me. Unlike

Job's friends, he didn't try to talk me out of anything I was feeling. He simply joined me and honored my mourning, letting his own tears fall and helping to remind me of God's presence. So now, my friends, I would like to share with you a prayer of lament for the suffering or loss you experience in your own life, for the sin in your own heart that has caused pain to others, for the pain of the world in which you participate. You may offer this prayer alone, with a trusted friend or with a small group.

Mary's Lament

Begin with a spoken prayer, a psalm, a dedication of this time. Then play some evocative music to help you begin to break through the numbness of your heart. Move gently to the music, letting your body soften its rigidity and the hardness of your heart begin to melt. Breathe deeply as you move. When you are ready, take a pillow into your arms and sit on the floor. For when we lament, the Scriptures call us to "Come down and sit in the dust...."[12]

Hold the pillow to your chest and begin to rock gently back and forth. After you are accustomed to this motion, begin to let out a small sighing sound as you exhale. Let your mind travel to the pain within your heart—a weakness you are grappling with, a burden of guilt, a weight of worry. With each sigh breathe out your pain. When you are ready, allow images of the world's pain and sin to enter your mind. Again, let your breath carry the cries that lie within you.

Your sighs may remain quiet and tender, or you may discover that once you give yourself permission to let down, your tears well up and spill over. Don't be afraid to sob. If you are in a group, you may even want to dedicate a certain part of your time to keening, wailing aloud with the whole group. *Don't worry if you feel a little awkward or if you don't feel deep grief at the moment. The Israelites prescribed times for grieving that did not necessarily match their emotional timing. Going through the motions paves a way to express the feelings when they do well up.*

Anger is part of grief. If you feel anger at the sins of humanity or even anger at God, feel free to strike the pillow or tear at it, just as the Israelites rent their garments. Take turns being with one another, to witness and honor and support each other's mourning.

When the time has come, spend time reflecting on your feelings by journal writing or drawing or sharing with another. You can end your time with a washing and/or anointing with scented oil, as the Israelites signaled the end of mourning by bathing and anointing. Close your lament with a prayer of thanksgiving and perhaps a song of praise. Cleansed and renewed, go forth to love and serve your God. Amen.

Dominic: What a powerful prayer, Mary! I, too, know the power of tears. When my journeying brought me to a hill overlooking a city, sometimes I could not help seeing the miseries unleashed by sin. The pain of my brothers and sisters moved me to tears, and I could not find words to express the anguish I felt. So I fell to the ground, prostrating myself before my sole Help and weeping, using the inspired words of the Psalmist: "I am utterly bowed down and prostrate; / all day long I go around mourning."[13]

Prostrate yourselves before God, dear friends, and plead for mercy. "If you cannot weep for your own sins, because you have none, still there are many sinners to be directed to God's mercy and love, and the apostles and prophets prayed for them with great groanings, and for their sake too Jesus wept when he saw them, and similarly the holy David, saying, 'I saw the half-hearted and I pined away.'"[14]

In the early days of the Order I described the gift of tears as a "violent affection involving repentance, compassion, and sorrow because of sin."[15] My brothers sometimes told me that I had awakened them in the night with these piercing cries: "O, Lord, be merciful to your people. What will become of poor sinners?"[16]

So you see, my tears led me to the great desire to bring about a change of heart in those around me. Dear retreatants, you will come to see that contemplating— really uniting ourselves with Jesus—causes us to turn away from selfishness and to burn with desire for the salvation of others, working toward that goal in prayer, penance and good works.

Ignatius: Throughout much of my life, the Lord has blessed me, too, with the gift of holy tears. When I reflect on all of my sins, all those whom I have injured and the offenses I have flung in God's face, I am deeply grieved. Gestures of repentance and the blessed gift of tears help me to express the emotion that stirs within me. Like a boiling pot that will explode if the lid is not removed, so these feelings must find their way into our prayer. Prayerful, postured repentance, overflowing into holy tears, expresses with the help of the Holy Spirit what could not otherwise be expressed.

Mary: So often our spirits feel lifted and our hearts cleansed when we allow ourselves to cry. And after the storm, we find ourselves in a clearing. In this clearing I invite you now to the prayer of forgiveness.

Dominic: And for many, this is the hardest prayer of all.

Ignatius: That's right, Dominic. For many, the wounds we have spoken of earlier run so deep that it seems a tragedy to forgive. We want to ask instead: "Where is justice?" We want to demand justice!

Mary: And yet, we are challenged to remember the loving words my Son spoke as he hung on the cross, "Father, forgive them; for they do not know what they are doing."[17] We are all called to forgive.

Ignatius: Forgiving is an act of courage, and it often transforms our relationships. Yet it is a mistake to confuse forgiveness with reconciliation. Sometimes the people who have wounded us deeply never move beyond their hurtful ways. It is not healthy to continue subjecting ourselves to injury. This is certainly the case for those in abusive relationships: They need to separate from their abusers and can never be reconciled. Still, forgiveness can liberate us from old wounds. Whenever we hold onto resentment, festering anger and hardness burden our hearts. When we forgive as Jesus forgives, our hearts are set free to love again.

Mary: Ignatius, will you lead our retreatants in the prayer of forgiveness?

Ignatius: Yes. Pilgrim friends, allow yourself at least fifteen minutes of prayer time. Turn off the phone. Dim the lights. Shut the door to your room. Protect yourself so that you can go deeply into some vulnerable places within. For this is the beauty of this kind of prayer: It allows subconscious truth that the conscious mind suppresses to rise to the surface, like smoke from a fire.

Don't force the meditation. Let whatever comes to your mind have its say. Trust that Jesus will reveal his love to you.

Ignatius' Forgiveness Meditation[18]

Sit up straight in a comfortable chair. Take time to feel your feet on the floor. Become aware of your back resting against the chair. Breathe deeply. Take in all the strength and hope that you need. Exhale all that is not of God.

Imagine that Jesus comes into the room and stands before you. His face is radiant with light and beautiful beyond description. Look into his eyes. Are you able to sense his love for you?

Jesus asks permission to look inside your heart. If you say yes, his loving eyes search every inch of your heart, every corner of your soul. He looks without judgment or condemnation, with love and understanding. Nothing is hidden from him who loves you without limit. Are there places of your heart that you feel like hiding? If so, speak to Jesus about these.

Speak to him of your life's choices. Tell him of the sadness of your life. Reveal to him the secret shame and the burdens of guilt that chain your soul.

Perhaps you see in his eyes tears of compassion. Are you able to sense the depth of his love? Lay down the burden of your sin. Surrender to his ocean of mercy.

Jesus again asks permission of you, this time to touch your heart. If you say yes, he reaches out and places his strong but gentle hand in the center of your chest. Place one of your own hands over his wounded hand in the center of your chest.

Jesus invites you to place your other hand on his heart. (You may extend your arm and hand to help your

*imagination picture this scene.) Feel the power of his love
flowing into you. Breathe deeply of this love. And as you
exhale, picture all the fear and shame of your life being
expelled by the power of his presence in your life. "[B]y his
bruises we are healed."*[19]

*Jesus turns and looks into the corner of the room. You
see someone standing there whom you need to forgive or
from whom you need to ask forgiveness. Who is this
person? This person may be living or dead, but there is
some wall between the two of you that the Lord wants to
break down.*

*The other approaches Jesus, and you see that Jesus loves
that person with the same gentle intensity with which he
loves you. Jesus places his other hand on his or her heart.*

*Breathe deeply of the love that flows into you from the
heart of our God. Jesus also invites this person to place his
or her hand on his heart, right beside your hand. Are you
able to let this person be with Jesus beside you?*

*Once again look into the eyes of Jesus to find the
strength you need. Now look into the eyes of the other and
pray silently or aloud, "I forgive you because Jesus forgives
you. I love you because Jesus loves you."*

*Look back into Jesus' eyes for the strength you need to
proceed. Breathe deeply of Jesus' strength.*

*Once again look into the eyes of the other and pray, "I
forgive you because Jesus forgives you. I love you because
Jesus loves you."*

*Return your gaze to Jesus. Know that forgiveness, like
love, begins with an act of the will. You may need to repeat
this prayer many times before you feel your emotions
beginning to heal. We cannot force our feelings, but we can
invite the Holy Spirit to come within us by this simple act
of forgiveness.*

*For a third and final time return your gaze to the eyes
of the other. Let the Holy Spirit pray within you. "I forgive*

you because Jesus forgives you. I love you because Jesus loves you."

Now simply continue to breathe deeply and watch what Jesus does. Listen to what Jesus says, and do whatever he tells you.

When you sense your prayer of imagination coming to an end, conclude by speaking to Jesus about what you saw and heard, felt and realized.

For Reflection

- Am I willing to claim my weaknesses and my strengths? Am I willing to let God love me into healing?

- What are the pains I have inflicted on others, especially family members and those closest to me? How will I now be a healer of these pains?

- How do my everyday actions, such as making an effort to recycle or driving safely, show that I realize the chain effects of sin? How do I enter into the work of preparing the way for the fullness of the Kingdom?

Closing Prayer

'Lord, Have Mercy'

As our closing prayer, we combine the ancient cry for mercy—the Kyrie—with the simplest of human gestures, opening and closing our hands. The following meditation may be used for private prayer or during public devotions. (During public devotion, feel free to alter this prayer by opening and closing your hands while they remain in front of you at waist level.)

*Whether you are standing or sitting, feel your feet
rooted to the earth. Rest secure in a sacred place of blessing.
Breathe deeply of God's love.*

*Take a moment to look at the palms of your open hands.
Hold in one hand all of what makes you who you are. Hold
there the blessings of your life. Give thanks for all the
people, events and gifts with which God has graced you.*

*Also call to mind the ways in which you have not lived
according to God's plan. Hold in your other hand the sin of
your life. Let this hand curl into a fist around your defiance,
for with every sin we close our hearts and block the healing
action of God's holy will. Now let both your arms drop to
your sides, one hand open and one in a fist, and pray:*

Lord, you have called us to be a people of faith. We
believe that you have the words of everlasting life.
And yet our faith is weak. Lord, we believe; help our
unbelief.

Lord, have mercy!
Now bend your arms and lift them to your waist.

Christ, you have called us to be a people of hope. We
remember how Moses brought water from the rock,
how you offered the Samaritan woman living water.
And yet we have not quenched the thirst of our
hearts in you. We have drunk from the empty
cisterns of our own discouragement.

Christ, have mercy!
Raise your arms and hands to the heavens.

Lord, you have called us to be a people of love. We
have felt your love flowing through us, but we have
loved too feebly. Called to be your disciples, we
confess we have lived anonymously.

Lord, have mercy!

As a sign of yielding to the healing mercy of Jesus, slowly lower your arms to waist level and fully open both palms. Let your heart and soul, mind and body open to the great healing love of our God.

May Almighty God have mercy on us, forgive us our sins, and bring us to life everlasting. Amen.

Notes

[1] A paraphrase of this story can be found in the collection *Challenge 2000, A Daily Meditation Program Based on the Spiritual Exercises of Saint Ignatius* by Mark Link, S.J. (Allen, Tex.: Tabor Publishing, 1993), pp. 112-113.

[2] Luke 15:18.

[3] William A. Barry, S.J., *Finding God in All Things* (Notre Dame, Ind.: Ave Maria Press, 1991), p. 63.

[4] This blessing is based on several scriptural passages, some of which include: mind—Philippians 4:17, 2 Corinthians 3:14; ears—Psalm 81:11, Matthew 13:14-17; eyes—Mark 8:18, Matthew 6:22-23; tongue—Psalm 139:4, James 3:4-5; throat—Psalm 69:3, Romans 3:13; neck—Deuteronomy 31:27, Jeremiah 17:23; heart—Ezekiel 36:27, Luke 2:51; stomach—Romans 16:18, Philippians 3:19; sexuality—2 Samuel 11, Romans 6:19-20; rump—Exodus 29:22-25, Leviticus 8:25; hands—Psalm 63:4, Matthew 19:15; feet—Psalm 22:16, Isaiah 52:7.

[5] See Genesis 32:22-32.

[6] See *Victim, Survivor, Celebrant: The Healing Journey from Childhood Sexual Abuse*, by Roberta Nobleman (St. Meinrad, Ind.: Abbey Press, 1994), pp. 140-141.

[7] See Revelation 11:15—12:17.

[8] Matthew 23:23-24.

[9] Psalm 51:1-15.

[10] See Judith 4:11-13.

[11] Psalm 88:1-3.

[12] Isaiah 47:1a.

[13] Psalm 38:6.

[14] Simon Tugwell, *The Nine Ways of Prayer of St. Dominic* (Dublin, Ireland: Dominican Publications, 1978), pp. 18-20.

[15] Marie-Humbert Vicaire, O.P., *The Genius of Saint Dominic: A Collection of Study-Essays*, ed. Peter B. Lobo, O.P. (Nagpur, India: Dominican Publications, 1981), p. 105.

[16] Ibid., p. 3.

[17] Luke 23:34.

[18] This meditation is inspired by another prayer of forgiveness in *Forgiveness and Inner Healing* by Betty Tapscott and Father Robert DeGrandis, S.S.J. (Santa Barbara, Calif.: Queenship Publishing, 1980).

[19] Isaiah 53:5.

DAY FOUR
Walking With Christ

Coming Together in the Spirit

A young boy suffered from a terrible fear of the dark. He was an only child, well loved by his parents. No amount of patient reasoning could deter the panic that befell him when it was time to go to his bedroom alone.

He brushed and rebrushed his teeth. He scrubbed his face and hands repeatedly, like a surgeon preparing to enter the operating room. His bedtime stories and evening prayers went on endlessly. He used every excuse in the book to avoid facing the terror of the night. Worn to a frazzle, his parents tried once again to reason with him. "You know, Mikey, there is nothing to be afraid of because God is always with you," they said.

Not to be out-theologized, the boy retorted, "I don't want God. I want somebody with skin on!"[1]

Defining Our Thematic Context

All of us long for a God with "skin on." Jesus is the answer to our longing. In our retreat we have been praying for the ability to hold two great truths before us: We are loved, and we are sinners. To ignore one or the other is to veer away from the truth of God's word.

Today we begin to contemplate the Incarnation, the Word made flesh. Jesus is the greatest revelation of who God is and how much God loves us.

We are called to walk with Christ, our strong and victorious King, and to receive Christ, a poor and humble child. We pray for the grace to humble our hearts and follow where Jesus will lead.

Opening Prayer

Bethlehem-Bound

Dominic, Ignatius, Mother Mary, come with me to the manger.
I want to grow young again, and I cannot go alone.
Each year I grow old in my soul. I don't mean wise—
The eyes of my heart darken. The ears of my spirit harden.
The racing pace and the tension of time,
disappointment in others, anger in me, fear of this and hurt from that—
Like some old veteran smarting over scars, I feel my wounds.
I am bent with grief at the pity of our lives.

But he comes! O yes, he comes! This little one.
He smiles at you. He laughs at me. We know he knows our hearts.
He calls us to kneel, not in a perfumed palace
but a stench-filled cave of wonder.
O the joy of such kneeling!
For it is here we are reborn into youth.

This little one with tiny hands and innocent eyes,
smiling and laughing at our grown-up fears—

See now how he still reaches out to us, so tenderly,
    playfully,
so lovingly he tears away our masks, like a child
    unwrapping gifts.

Come now, my friends, let us go down to the "House
    of Bread."
Bethlehem bound, let our souls be fed like hungry
    farm animals,
feasting from this manger of hope.
For behold a God who comes to us unprotected,
Wrapped only in swaddling, soft as a fleece.

We are not so innocent or so unprotected.
And yet you and I, my friends, my mentors,
this day we are invited
to wonder, to witness the birth of this babe, this gift of
    our Savior!
In the cave of our hearts, this Christ Child still waits
    for our kiss.

O Jesus, to be such a lamb gazing at hidden glory,
or even a dumb ox kneeling in silent wonder!
I want to grow young again, and I cannot go alone.
Dominic, Ignatius, Mother Mary, come with me to the
    manger.

RETREAT SESSION FOUR

Ignatius: Welcome, pilgrims. I trust your prayer is feeding
you well. Today we wish to take you closer to the heart of
our Christian faith, the Incarnation. What incomprehensi-
ble mystery is hidden inside that four-syllable word! God

becomes one of us. Even here amid the angels and saints, I still marvel at the goodness of our God taking on human flesh, becoming one of us!

Dominic: The Albigensians against whom I battled could never really take to heart the truth of this mystery. That the infinite God would become like us in all things but sin is indeed cause for wonder.

Ignatius: It is this God who calls us, invites us into the fray. Let me try to make this invitation seem more real to you: Close your eyes and imagine the most compelling personality, the most gifted individual you have ever met or imagined meeting.[2] Imagine the most magnetic personality you can—a rock star, a movie star, a religious leader, an athlete, an artist, a poet. Do you see a historical figure, perhaps a politician—

Dominic: Oh, now we are dreaming!

Ignatius: Yes, this is a fantasy. But this leader speaks of a desire to be of service to all, to bring everyone joy and peace, health and happiness. This is a nonviolent, holy crusade.

The leader warns you that it's likely to be tough going for a while. The food will, at times, be meager. The blankets will wear thin. The computers will go down. The air conditioning will blow out in the summer and the water heaters spring leaks in the winter. Many will fall away and become discouraged. Many will taunt you and call you a fool for following. This will not be an easy climb. But, the leader promises to be with you, no matter what.

Now imagine that the leader, this hero, walks up to you, looks you right in the eyes and calls you by name.

The leader puts a very simple question to you: "Will you follow me? Will you serve my cause?"

Dominic: How could any sane person refuse such an offer?

Ignatius: That's precisely my point! They wouldn't refuse. So if we will follow the offer of an earthly hero, even to the death, how much more will the invitation of our God and king move us?

Mary: Well, my sons, there were days when I said yes. But, I must admit, there were also days when I said no.

Ignatius: You said no, Mary? What do you mean?

Mary: Well, like the time when Joseph came to tell me about the census. After all my days of trusting in the midst of the unknown, suddenly something cracked inside of me. "No! No! No!" I cried out. "My God, accept my anger! Do not turn away from me. Send your armies to destroy Caesar Augustus and all his pompous census-takers, too! Is it Joseph's fault for being from Bethlehem? Is this how you treat the mother of your son?" I was shaking. I just couldn't understand.

I tried to pray, but I was overwhelmed with emotion. I wanted to go outside to the field where so often my soul had sung to God, but I was too distraught.

My eye caught the shape of an olive branch—the one Joseph had hung on the wall for beating the rugs. I unhooked it, and took up the rug from the floor and ran out to the field.

I threw all of my rage into the rug, striking, beating. "Why must we travel *now* when I am so heavy with child?" Thwack! A cloud of dust rose up. "How shall I journey? How shall I give birth without my mother or the midwives to help? What does Joseph know about delivering babies?" Thwack!—another cloud of dust. "My God, I don't want to give birth alone! I should have asked your angel friend what was required of me before I said yes!" Thwack, thwack! "Besides, if this is your Son, why don't you take care of him—and me? Yahweh, do you hear me? Answer me!" Thwack! "Answer me!" Thwack! "Answer me!" Thwack!

Ignatius: Mother Mary, you are so honest with us. What human being does not struggle to accept God's holy will? Even you did!

Mary: Dear Ignatius, Jesus struggled in the garden at Gethsemane. How could I not struggle when my life was at risk? We must teach these seekers that it's not feeling that's sinful; what people sometimes do with their feelings brings sin into the world. My expression that day was the movement of my heart to bring myself into alignment with God. It was more than anger or lament. It was my psalm of protest. How could God give me this trial? Gone was my innocent trusting.

And yet, somehow, I knew enough to take my anger to prayer. As I did, God carved out in me an even deeper faith. And in the midst of my ranting, God did manage to get a word in edgewise. After my outburst, the cloud of dust that obscured my heart began to settle. In the silence after the storm I heard a still, small voice, like the whisper of the wind: "Mary, Mary,"

> Do not fear, for I have redeemed you;
> I have called you by name, you are mine.
> When you pass through the waters, I will be with you;
> and through the rivers, they shall not overwhelm you;
> when you walk through fire you shall not be burned,

and the flame shall not consume you.
For I am the LORD your God,
the Holy One of Israel, your Savior.[3]

Finally, my heart broke open. Under the blue skies of Palestine, I once again opened my hands. "Yes, Lord. Lead me. Guide me. Take me where I need to go. I am your daughter. I put my life in your hands."

Dominic: I went through many moments of doubt and agony like that. It is comforting to know that your trust was not without trial. After all, are we not children of the new Israel? Remember Ignatius' reference to the story of Jacob in our previous day of prayer.

Ignatius: Limping on earth, that we might dance in heaven!

Dominic: Amen, Father!

Mary: Yes, I, too, needed to limp through the flames of my own fear and the river of my ranting and raving to know that even then, God would stay with me. And God did stay with me. Joseph stayed with me, too. Somehow we got to Bethlehem—but we walked into that city with nothing except the bread and lentils I had packed, and the swaddling clothes tucked into our donkey's satchel.

My contractions were growing intense. As night began to fall, I thought perhaps people would take pity on us, but doors slammed shut in our faces and we could hear the roar of laughter and drinking. Finally, one man (was his name Gabriel, too?) led us out back to the stable—a cave, really. In labor, I surrendered myself to the most ancient rituals, the most sacred liturgy.

I didn't know birth would be so much like death, dark and damp in the cave, my body on fire. Joseph made a bed for me there in the hay. As I lay breathing, my body was taken over by an ancient power—the force of an ocean, the strength of the wind that parted the waters of the Red Sea. I gave myself to the God of pounding surf and surging tides within me. And slowly, through rising waves and ever-widening door, my helpless child slipped into our world.

Amid all the blood and the bleating of the lambs, this new one came into our midst. I held him in my arms—face shining like the stars, angels singing in my ears. All memory of pain and protest faded as I beheld this brand-new face of God. I was flooded, I was transfixed, I was buoyant in a sea of love. I wanted to dance with the angels and sing with the stars and beckon the whole world to marvel with me at such mystery.

Shepherds came and wise men followed, full of wonder. I held this child against the drum of my chest, our hearts repeating some ancient dance made absolutely new. I prayed—"O child, you make me mother, and somehow I have made you child." This moment remains suspended in time, through centuries, through civilizations, through crèche and Christmas carol: the birth of Christ, the Incarnation.

Ignatius: Thank you, Mother, for telling us of his birth. Your reflections help me to appreciate more fully this mystery so far beyond words.

Dear pilgrims, our Lady appeared to me when I was convalescing in my home at Loyola. She was holding the child Jesus in her arms. From the moment I saw her and her Son my soul was flooded with a grace for which I shall always be grateful. From that moment on I never seriously sinned against the virtue of purity.[4]

When I wrote the *Constitutions of the Society of Jesus* and carried on my duties as superior general of the Order,

I had a beautiful portrait of our Blessed Lady over my desk. It was a favorite painting with her holding the child Christ in her arms.

Mary: I remember the portrait well. "Our Lady of the Writing Desk," it is now called. I remember praying with you as you prayed with me and my Son. It is God's will that all my children come to know the great humility of Jesus.

Dominic: Paul put it well in his Letter to the Philippians:

> Let the same mind be in you that was in Christ Jesus,
> who, though he was in the form of God,
> did not regard equality with God
> as something to be exploited,
> but emptied himself,
> taking the form of a slave,
> being born in human likeness.[5]

Ignatius: If we are to advance in the spiritual life, we must let go of our pride and take these inspired words to heart. So much of Basque and Spanish culture was filled with a machismo that prompted men constantly to attempt to prove their manhood. My own conversion was a stripping away of this false armor so that the true armor—Christ's love for us—would emerge.

Dominic: Perhaps women are better than men in discerning the power of tenderness. The women the Lord first gave me as my followers helped me to understand the gentle love of our Mother and of Brother Jesus through their own example.

Mary: It is the Father's design that women be the bearers of new life in this world. Remember that my Son told us that we all must become like little children if we are to enter the Kingdom. But come, Ignatius, and guide our readers' imagination to the cave at Bethlehem.

Ignatius: From the earliest days of my conversion I longed to traverse the land where our Lord walked. And, once I was there, I wanted never to leave. But the Lord taught me that through imagination I could return to the Holy Land again and again—to Calvary, to the Sea of Galilee, to Bethlehem.

Mary: Lead us, son, in the kind of meditation that the Lord taught you so long ago in the caves at Manresa.

Dominic: Yes, guide our hearts and imaginations to the cave where even to this day, our gentle Mother and her Son wait for us.

Ignatius' Meditation: 'Into the Cave'[6]

Ignatius: Fellow pilgrims, breathe deeply and relax. Recall that we are in the presence of all of the heavenly court. Dominic and I are with you, as are all the saints. Your guardian angel stands a silent watch over you, and countless hosts of angels wait to do God's bidding. Now pray with me:

> Mary, reveal yourself to us. Mother us lovingly. Share with us your Son. Share with us the treasure from your heart, those mysteries stored up and pondered in contemplation throughout the centuries. Guide our hearts to Jesus.
>
> *Now breathe in the love that the Lord longs to give you. Imagine that the chair that you are sitting on slowly begins*

to rise. Feel yourself relaxed and unafraid. The roof opens and you rise up into the open air. Sense yourself protected inside a sphere of grace, a sphere of blessing that begins to move eastward to the ocean. You and your trusted companions are now traveling at incredible speeds—totally relaxed, protected and graced.

You travel across the Atlantic, across the Mediterranean to the shore of Israel, to David's city, Bethlehem. Your sphere of blessing begins to descend through the clouds. The roof of the Church of the Nativity opens up and you find yourself lowered into the cave below it.

The sphere disappears and you are now face-to-face with Joseph, Mary and the newborn babe, Jesus. Feel yourself welcome here.

What does the child Jesus look like? Notice his little face, the softness of his skin, his tiny arms and toes. Perhaps Mary smiles at you and invites you to hold the child in your arms.

Reach out and hold this divine child. Love this child and let him love you. Open your heart to his.

Here there is no need to posture or pretend. Let heart speak to heart. Rock him back and forth or lift him to the sky. Cuddle him, kiss him. Love this child who first loved you. Unfold to him the secrets of your heart. Tell him what your heart longs to pray. He trusts you enough to give himself into your arms; trust this child with the burden that you have carried long enough.

Surrender to him all that robs you of life. Offer to him those you cannot forgive because of the hurt they have caused you. Entrust to him your guilt, regret, fear and shame.

Let this child love you into freedom. In holy tears and holy laughter, let him love you into life.

You may wish to touch the center of his tender chest,

near his heart. Feel that heart beating with love for you. Imagine him touching your own heart, massaging your heart with love.

What do you need to ask of this child? Is there something that he asks of you?

Look to Joseph. Is there something he tells you or does for you, or something you ask of him?

Look to Mary. Is there something she tells you or does for you, or something you ask of her?

The time for your departure draws near. Offer to return the child to his mother. Does she invite you to raise him as your own?

Trust what she tells you. And carry Jesus' presence or the memory of his presence within your heart.

Return to your chair with your trusted companions. Once again the chair begins to rise; it lifts you through the ceiling of the cave. You rise into the clouds in a circle of grace, a sphere of protection.

You begin the long journey home. Traveling at incredible speeds, across the Mediterranean, across the ocean, westward toward your home—to your state, your city, your house. The sphere descends through the clouds like a great balloon. The ceiling of your residence opens. And you find yourself home again in your chair with your trusted companion beside you.

Before you open your eyes, continue to breathe deeply; call to mind what you have just experienced. Before the memory of this prayer escapes you, recall what you heard and saw and felt that most strengthened you.

Did anything come up from your subconscious that confused or frightened you?

Is there some part of the prayer that you will want to explore in more depth at another time, or with someone else present?

Before you end this meditation, offer three prayers: Take

a moment to tell the Blessed Mother what this prayer has
meant to you. Then speak to Jesus about what you have
seen, heard or felt. Finally, speak to our Abba *in heaven*
about what fills your heart at this moment. Amen! Amen!

Dominic: Well prayed, brother. I wish I had received the help of your guidance during my lifetime.

Ignatius: And I wish I had received the benefit of your preaching!

Mary: And I delight to have both of you as my sons. Yes, we need to pray with our whole selves. So much of our prayer is stilted and crippled.

Dominic: I also have been graced with an understanding of the mystery of the birth of our holy Lord. One night as I was pondering the joyful mysteries of the Nativity and the Presentation, I was blessed with a vision that intensified my belief that Jesus, God-with-us, came to save and not to condemn.

I glanced at the other end of the dormitory and saw three women enter. The one in the middle was a venerable lady of greater beauty and dignity than the other two. One of the two was carrying a beautiful shining vessel and the other a holy water sprinkler, which she handed to the lady in the center.

The lady sprinkled the brethren and blessed them. Then she said: "I am the one you call upon each evening. When you say, 'Turn then, most gracious Advocate,' I prostrate myself before my Son and ask him to preserve this Order."

Then I was caught up in spirit before God. I saw the Lord and the Blessed Virgin sitting at his right. As I looked around, I could see religious of all the orders but my own before the throne of God. I began to weep bitterly and stood apart, not daring to approach the Lord and his Mother. Then our Lady motioned for me to come near. But I did not dare until the Lord also called me.

I cast myself down before them, weeping bitterly. The Lord told me to rise, and when I did, asked me, "Why are you weeping so?"

"I am weeping," I told him, "because I see all the other orders here but no sign of my own."

Then the Lord said to me, "Do you want to see your Order?"

I answered, "Yes, Lord." So the Blessed Virgin opened the cloak she was wearing and spread it out before me. It seemed vast enough to cover the entire heaven, and under it I saw a large multitude of my brethren.

After that, the vision disappeared, but I felt my body arching heavenward as my body and soul surged toward God in thanksgiving and praise, in total love, desire, offering for the saving divine love.

It always amazes me how diverse the gifts of the Spirit are.

Mary: Yes, when we surrender to the Lord, we glorify God in our spirits and in our flesh.

Dominic: And now, Mother, would you speak again to lead our retreatants in a holy meditation? We all need to be held in love by you.

Ignatius: Yes, Mother, speak to their pilgrim hearts and reveal to them something of what you revealed to Dominic and me.

Mary: My pilgrim friends, I see so many of you carrying the weight of endless responsibilities in your day-to-day lives. I long for the moments when you lay down your burdens and let me hold you in my arms.

I know some of you carry deep mother wounds—even Jesus and I had conflicts to negotiate! And yet God offers us all the lap of a loving Mother, with no strings attached. Because God has offered me so much love, my heart is overflowing with that bounty, and this gift I offer to you. Come pray this meditation with me. I open my arms to hold you.

With Mary, Mother of Mercy

When you are ready, sit comfortably and bring your attention to your breath. Draw your breath in slowly and let your belly expand. Then as you exhale, let your breath go, releasing. Continue breathing deeply.

Now put your hand on your heart and feel the life pulse inside of you—the ongoing rhythm of life. Listen to your heart. In this moment, what grace does your heart need? Is there some desire buried inside that you now have the gentleness to uncover? Perhaps there is a child in you that carries a special need.

Now call upon me, Mary, your Mother of Mercy. Invite me to be with your need. See me, a gentle presence standing before you, my body warm and radiant with inner light. Let me see you now, exactly as you are. Let me see your longing to be loved. Perhaps you would like to reach out to me now, opening your hands to healing. Let me love you.

With your invitation, I come closer to you. My heart cannot help but go out to you, the child I have loved all along and have been waiting to welcome. See me reaching out to hold you, offering you my mother's embrace. Perhaps you would like to shift your position and let yourself settle into my arms. Let yourself be my child exactly as you are, whatever you are feeling in this moment. Trust me enough to hold you in tenderness.

Is there something troubling you now? Some cross you have had to bear? Let me know your story. Lay down your burden. Like Jesus surrendering his spirit, as you breathe out, give me your fear, your anger, your pain, whatever feelings and memories well up in you. My arms are big enough to contain all that you give over to me. Let me rock you now, or touch your cheek, or stroke your hair. Listen as I sing my love to you, a lullaby for my holy child.

Open your ears now to the message I have for you—the gentle words of comfort, encouragement or tenderness that you need to hear. Let me speak to you.

I have been waiting for this moment, the opening of your heart, to share with you the healing love you desire. Remember how I once nourished my son with the same tenderness I give to you. Breathe in the grace of my love; like a mother's sweet milk, drink in my gift to you. As you exhale, breathe out the old unworthiness. No need for that. I have chosen you as my own. I accept you, I embrace you as you are.

I listen to you with loving-kindness. Now I invite my son, Jesus, to join us. See him drawing near to us, his heart on fire with love. Listen as I speak to my son, telling him all about you, my beloved child. I speak to him about your needs, and his love pours out to you. What word, what gesture, what gift does Jesus bring to you? Give yourself all the time you need to take in Jesus' love for you.

Like a baby who drinks until satisfied, let yourself drink until you are full. Then linger in our loving embrace. Is there anyone else you want to invite into this circle of light? If so, see that person joining our circle, enveloped in the love we share. What word, what gesture, what grace does my son share with your friend? What blessing do I give?

When you are ready, let your friend go, bearing the gift of our gathering. Breathe in again the fullness of our time together. Take a few moments to let your heart overflow in thanks for the blessing we have shared. What word or gesture of thanks do you give to Jesus? What gift of gratitude do you give to me?

In a dance between mother and child, let us bow to each other now, acknowledging the Christ we each carry. We send each other on our way, filled with the joy of our ongoing relationship, knowing that at any moment we can return to our loving embrace.

In reflection on our visit, take a few moments to recall the fruits of your prayer.

Dominic: I thank you, Mother. I felt your love during my lifetime. You brought me to Jesus and gave me the strength I needed to face ridicule, persecution, hunger and fatigue. When our hearts and souls are well fed, we have the strength we need to face the world.

Mary: That is my mission: to bring all to Jesus! I invite our retreatants at this point to open up their Scriptures and to reflect upon their favorite Gospel scenes.

Ignatius: As you pray these scenes, I encourage you to enter into them with all the powers of your imagination. Use all your senses to help them come alive. Place yourself inside the scene, as we just did with the meditations on the Nativity.

Dominic: You may also wish to embody the prayer with the use of creative gesture and movement. Let me give you just one example of how this may be done.

I love the Sermon on the Mount, in which Jesus gives

us the Beatitudes as a path to balance and joy. Join us, friends, in praying these Beatitudes from that holy sermon:[7]

Dominic's Meditation on the Beatitudes

'Blessed are the poor in spirit....'
> *Kneel with hands open and extended, as you realize that being poor in spirit means that you must not give the highest value to the material things of life.*

'Blessed are those who mourn....'
> *Fall to the ground in prostration as you hear Jesus promise that those who mourn will be comforted. Place your sadness in his care and wait in his love for comfort.*

'Blessed are the meek....'
> *Imagine yourself before a cross. Stand with your arms at your sides, facing the cross, as you are called to be meek—to face troubles and suffer injuries without complaint or a spirit of revenge.*

'Blessed are those who hunger and thirst for righteousness....'
> *Stand and hold your arms straight out from your sides, evenly, strongly, as you ponder the fact that those who hunger and thirst for righteousness will be satisfied. Think about respecting the rights and property of others and working for justice for your brothers and sisters in specific ways.*

'Blessed are the merciful....'
> *Bring your hands up and out in a gesture of blessing as you recall that being merciful will obtain mercy. Bless someone who has hurt you and ask for God's mercy to heal your broken relationship.*

'Blessed are the pure in heart....'
> *Fold your hands over your heart and bow your head before the Lord. Examine your thoughts, words and actions to see if you are doing all things with the intention of pleasing God.*

'Blessed are the peacemakers....'
> *Stretch out your arms in welcoming love to all, knowing that the peacemakers are the children of God.*

'Blessed are those who are persecuted for righteousness' sake....'
> *Arch your body heavenward in full assurance, knowing that if you suffer persecution here, your reward in heaven will be great.*

Ignatius: Thank you, Dominic. The blessedness Jesus speaks of is not unbalanced giddiness; rather, it is happiness in trusting in his promises.

Mary: We all can taste of this happiness, Ignatius! Remember, though, that it wasn't long before the crowds began to dwindle and the time of the Passion drew near. Remember that disciples must follow the same road. Place those promises firmly in your hearts in your days of enthusiasm, for there will be days when you will need to recall them for the strength to continue the journey.

For Reflection

- What favorite Scripture passage can I pray using the tools of imagination and embodiment? How can I bring this to my life?

■ In what ways will I embody the image of Mary, Mother of Mercy, for my family and my community?

Closing Prayer

The Our Father

Join us now in the prayer that Jesus himself has taught us:

Opening Stance

Begin by holding your hands before you. Simply look at your hands, which are uniquely your own. Through prayerful imagination, imagine that you hold in one hand some gift from God for which you are particularly grateful. This gift may be a person or persons, things or spiritual gifts you have received. Let yourself feel gratitude for what God has already given. Hold in the other hand an empty space for a gift from God for which you pray. For what does your heart cry out this day?

'Our Father...'

Present both of these, the gifts you have received and the gifts you seek, to the God Jesus called Abba. *Entrust yourself to the God who loves us more fully and more completely than any earthly mother or father could ever love.*

'Who art in heaven...'

Lift your gifts to this God who dwells in unapproachable mystery, to the God who always exceeds our expectations. This God of mystery dwells not in some distant universe, but is eternally present to us.

'Hallowed be thy name;...'

Now lower your hands to a place just in front of your heart,

*palms slightly cupped and facing each other, fingers
pointing to the sky. Leave an empty space between your
hands, enough room for the Holy Spirit to slip in, for the
place where God dwells within our hearts is holy, hallowed
ground.*

'Thy kingdom come;...'

*Stretch one arm forward, palm up, into an unknown future.
Yearn, stretch, desire, imagine, envision a world totally
surrendered to God.*

'Thy will be done...'

*Stretch the other arm forward in a two-handed,
wholehearted surrender to God.*

'On earth...'

*Round your arms before you, embracing the earth and its
people. Hold the sacredness of life in all its many forms.*

'As it is in heaven...'

*Once again lift your arms, looking beyond yourself and
your own needs.*

'Give us this day our daily bread;...'

*Bring your hands cupped together just in front of your
mouth, as if holding a small rice bowl. Pray in communion
with the billions of people on this planet who go to bed
hungry each night. Pray in communion with all those who
hunger for more than earthly bread. Pray for what we need
to sustain us today.*

'And forgive us our trespasses;...'

*Now lift your right hand and let your palm pass in front of
your own face in a gesture of loving forgiveness. Believe
that Jesus died to free us from our sins. Accept the Lord's
love and merciful kindness. Do not cling to your guilt and
shame.*

| Our Father... | who art in heaven... | Hallowed be thy name... | Thy kingdom come... | thy will be done... |

| On earth... | As it is in heaven... | Give us this day our daily bread... | And forgive us our trespasses... | As we forgive those who trespass against us... |

And lead us not into temptation... And deliver us from evil... For the kingdom and the power and the glory are yours now and forever.

'As we forgive those who trespass against us;...'
Turn and face your neighbor. (If you are doing this prayer
alone, imagine someone standing beside you.) Let this
person symbolize all those people in your life with whom
you need to be reconciled. Now let your open right hand
slowly pass in front of the other person's face as you forgive
them. Let your neighbor do this same gesture with you. The
easy part is doing the gesture and saying the words. The
hard part is letting go of the unforgiveness. The painful part
is letting our hearts be softened.

'And lead us not into temptation,...'
Form your hands into fists and cross your arms over your
chest. Feel the weight of the chains that bind you.

'But deliver us from evil...'
Now open and straighten your hands and arms to own the
far greater power and strength that free us...

'For the kingdom, the power and the glory are yours...'
...if we but join hands and hearts with one another and lift
them in joyful praise to our God.

'Now and forever.'
Lifting our faces to the heavens:

Amen.
Breathe in God's love. So be it. Amen!

Notes

[1] The original source of this story is unknown. The retelling is
original to the authors.

[2] This meditation is based on St. Ignatius' Kingdom Meditation,
Spiritual Exercises, #92, p. 43.

[3] Isaiah 43:1b-3a.

[4] *St. Ignatius' Own Story*, trans. William J. Young, S.J. (Chicago:

Loyola University Press, 1980), p. 11.

[5] Philippians 2:5-7.

[6] Based on the audiocassette *Treasures of the Heart: Meditations With Mary, Our Mother of Mercy*, by J. Michael Sparough, S.J., and Betsey Beckman. Music by Bobby Fisher. Cincinnati, Ohio: St. Anthony Messenger Press, 1994.

This meditation may be effectively read to another person who prays it. You may also find it helps to record this and other meditations in this retreat on cassette in your own voice.

[7] Matthew 5:1-10.

DAY FIVE
Embracing the Cross

Coming Together in the Spirit

Edina, a twelve-year-old from war-torn Bosnia, wrote a letter to all children throughout the world that relates some of the suffering she has endured. While staying in Serbian-held territory, she and her mother were put on a list for liquidation. At that point she began to experience terror and the unrelenting sort of suffering that only people under siege can comprehend. She asks us to be her brothers and sisters in peace by understanding her experience of the cross: "I want you to know our suffering, the children of Sarajevo. I am still young, but I feel that I have experienced things that many grown-ups will never know."

When we live "normal" lives, Edina reminds us, we take so much for granted. "While you are eating your fruit and your sweet chocolate and candy, over here we are plucking grass to survive."[1]

As Edina points out, we can enjoy the movies or listen to our favorite music while those in war-torn countries are hiding in basements without electricity, listening only to the whine of rockets and the cries of friends and families in fear. While stepping into the shower is a daily routine for most of us, those in Edina's circumstance pray that God will send rain so they will have some water to drink.

Defining Our Thematic Context

There is no more poignant image of human suffering or of God's love for us than the crucified Christ. To gaze in loving contemplation on the Son of God in agony is to confront the horror of sin and the immensity of God's unconditional love.

The cross of Christ is the ultimate expression of the body at prayer. It is to this cross that we must come. Here there are no easy answers to the tragic suffering and the radical injustice of human hatred. Our Christian faith provides no quick fixes, only an eternal promise: "I am with you always...."[2]

Opening Prayer

The Crucifixion

Mother Mary, Brother Dominic and Father Ignatius,
Stand with strength beside me during this day.
For I need to come face-to-face
with the Lord of love
in this place of pain, confusion and loss.
Pray with me, good directors, and teach me
to look with courage toward the cross
and to cry out in faith from the depths of my soul.
In truth, Lord,
your care, your eyes, your always being within me
fooled me,
and I opened myself completely.
I learned your words, studied your ways,
embraced your family as my own.
And now, look,
you're asking me to go still further.

How can love invade, probe, pierce,
break, drill, drive and gore?
More!
Yet, Lord, I believe in your love for me.
So give me this bitter drink to down.
I want the full cup from your hand, undiluted.
I want to drink it down.

RETREAT SESSION FIVE

Mary: My retreatants, are you ready to go into the hardest part of the journey? For now we come to the cross.

Ignatius: Remember, we will not leave you.

Dominic: We are by your side. Come with us.

Mary: By the time Jesus died, I was no longer a child. Books are written these days about times of passage in a woman's life—stories of women coming to grips with who they are after their children are grown and their youth has gone, stories of women going through menopause and discovering wisdom born of lifelong learnings and struggles, triumphs and mistakes. Calvary was my true coming of age. There, in the second half of my life, I had the greatest task of all—finding hope in that dark night.

Ignatius: But, Mary, how did you do it? How did you stand at the foot of the cross and watch Jesus' life being ripped away and spilled out in blood and water?

Mary: For me, Ignatius, it was a time of decision. My

whole life prepared me for that most terrible moment and helped me to recognize that even in the face of monstrous evil, I had a choice. There at the cross, I remembered the time when I shouted, "No, no, no!" when God called me to Bethlehem. I felt once again how frightened I was to give birth alone. Yet God brought radical new life through my pain. At thirteen I had been shocked by how much birth had seemed like death. Now I cried out that somehow death could bring about birth, that loving is never in vain.

I was not without desperation. In the earliest creed, your ancestors in the faith claimed that Jesus descended into hell after this death. Well, so did I. I stared the devil down. Once my son had been tempted; now it was my turn. The great face of evil tempted me to give in to despair, to resign myself to the senseless loss of life, to go along with the whims of people consumed with power and pseudo-righteousness. And yet the image of Abraham kept coming into my mind. The God who commanded Abraham somehow was telling me that I had to be willing to sacrifice my son. I longed for an ending such as Abraham found. I cried out for a ram to sacrifice instead of my son. Why must my son be the lamb?

Something gradually rose within me. During those endless hours of Jesus' torture and torment, trial and conviction, I knew that the only force more powerful than pain was love. I could not hide in fear. I could not deny my son as Peter had. I could not weep like the women on the way to Calvary. I had to stand. I had to stand in my power, my God-given grace. I had to stand and witness to love. My son needed my love in this moment more than ever before. With wave upon wave of grief consuming me, I sent wave upon wave of love to him.

I stood by my son while many fled, knowing he was victorious as he surrendered himself to the will of his

Father. This was the life for which God had prepared him; to that place beyond pain his spirit soared. I wanted to soar there with him, but it was not yet my time.

There was his body: the body I had once held in my arms so tenderly, bloody with birth; the child I had bathed and held fever-stricken to my heart; the boy who had laughed and played and run to me bearing tiny bouquets; the child I had to let go at twelve in the temple and whom I later watched as thousands gathered to hear his words and beg his healing touch. Now I took his body into my arms once more. With my heart pierced like his, I poured out my soul. I held him and rocked him; I sang to my baby, my boy, my son and my Savior one last time. I stroked him and my heart broke open.

My children, I call you to this courage. Deep within you lies the power to heal, to transform, to bring love out of brokenness. This is the love my son calls you to, the possibility he holds out to you. And so, I offer you now a meditation on forgiveness, a ritual of reconciliation.

Can you imagine Jesus' healing love coming to you— to that part of you of which you are most ashamed? These are the parts we so often want to hide, to deny. We are like Simon Peter, who at first refused to let his Master wash his feet. Yet, Jesus wants us to give ourselves with all our brokenness to his love. And then he wants us to carry this love to others, to offer ourselves in service to the world. How can we do this if we carry within us resentment or rejection, anger or animosity? We must be healed.

Mary's Foot-Washing Ritual [3]

Foot-washing is an act of devotion to share with others. My son told us, "So if I, your Lord and Teacher, have washed your feet, you also ought to wash one another's feet. For I have set you an example, that you also should do as I have done to you."[4] You will need another person to help you, someone willing to enter into a prayerful healing action with you. Pray about who can support you in this way, and then invite that person to accompany you on this journey.

When you have come together, have ready a pitcher with warm water, towels and a basin. Begin your healing ritual with a prayer and perhaps a song. Then read aloud the Scripture passage about Jesus washing the feet of his disciples (John 13:1-15). Next, spend a few moments meditating quietly to discover which part of you needs healing. Perhaps you carry a burden of guilt for a hurt you have inflicted on someone in your past. Maybe there is a weakness in your character that feels unlovable to you. Perhaps you have been wounded by someone in your life.

Once you each have a sense of what needs healing in this moment, decide whose feet will be washed first. Speak your woundedness to your friend and ask that you may be blessed and renewed by the love of my son. Seat yourself on a chair, and let your friend be Jesus for you. Let my son, through your friend, wash your feet tenderly, lovingly.

Notice if you find it hard to receive this great love. Let the healing love of Christ wash over you, penetrating the protective barriers you have constructed. When you are finished, stand anew on your feet, empowered to bring this same forgiveness to the world.

When it is your turn to be the Christ-figure, let your friend speak to you of his or her woundedness. Feel within you your call to be Christ. Sense Christ's love stirring in your heart. You may want to begin by touching your forehead lovingly to your friend's feet, bowing in humble reverence to this person you now serve and to the God embodied in the soul before you. Just as I washed my son's feet when he was an infant and held them, bloodstained, by the cross, take your friend's feet into your hands. One by one, wash them with gentle care.

If you feel so moved, let yourself speak to your friend words that Jesus might speak—words of encouragement, of forgiveness, of love. When you have finished, bow to your friend, acknowledging the sacredness you have shared.

Dominic: What a prayerful meditation, Mary! As Jesus washed his disciples' feet, he was preparing himself for his total surrender in death. Lead us now, in a procession of love with Jesus on the road to Calvary. Teach us the dance of courage and faithfulness, support and strength even in times of dire sadness, the Way of the Cross.

Mary: I will walk with you. Jesus will walk with you. But speak for us, Dominic, and show us how we can use some of your many ways of body-prayer to help move our spirits into step with my son.

Ignatius: Yes, Dominic. And may I suggest that we genuflect and recite the traditional prayer as we stop before each station along the way: "We adore you, O Christ, and we bless you, because by your holy cross you have redeemed the world." I have found these words and this action help me move from meditation to meditation.

Dominic: Yes, brother. Genuflecting frequently before an image of Christ crucified is one of the nine ways of prayer the brethren attributed to me. Many have found that same movement of help over the years. I would urge our friends to include this body prayer at the start of each station.

Dominic's Stations of the Cross

The First Station: Jesus Is Condemned to Death
Kneel with your hands at your sides, looking at Jesus.

Jesus, I see your swollen face, thorn-crowned head, clothes stained and sticking to open wounds. Yet even as Pilate gives his order and you stand to form a procession in the courtyard of the Praetorium with two other condemned men, I cannot see hate, resentment or shame in your eyes. You look at me with love.

The Second Station: Jesus Bears His Cross
Stand and position yourself in the form of a cross.

Once you moved quickly, gracefully. Now you move slowly. Pain distorts your face. You have had no sleep; nor have you eaten for some twelve hours. Yet for me you embrace that cross with all the strength you have, carrying forward my redemption.

The Third Station: Jesus Falls the First Time
Lie in prostration, beseeching God's mercy.

Weak from the torment of recent hours and loss of blood, your legs falter beneath you. You fall to the rough cobblestones. The soldiers whip you to keep you going. Yet you struggle to get up and move on because you want me to be free from the burden of sin.

The Fourth Station: Jesus Meets His Mother
Stand and extend your arms forward, reaching in love.

Spasms of pain rip through your body. Then you see your mother and your heart aches incredibly. You know she is suffering with you. She is not ashamed of you, for she understands that you have always done the will of God. Your love strengthens one another for the journey.

The Fifth Station: Jesus Is Helped by Simon
With both hands near your right shoulder, bow your torso, bearing the weight of the cross.

The soldiers, wanting to move the whole procession along more quickly, seize a Jew named Simon from the crowd and force him to help you drag the cross to

Calvary. Simon is a lot like me—grudgingly sharing your burden. How close we are to salvation at times without even realizing it!

The Sixth Station: Veronica Wipes the Face of Jesus
Kneel, placing your hands gently over your face.

A woman, filled with compassion at the sight of you, comes forth from the crowd. She takes her veil and gently places it over your face, to offer some solace. Can I recognize your bloody face in those who crowd around me each day? Can I reach out with something of my own to help another? Will you leave the imprint of your love on my heart when I do?

The Seventh Station: Jesus Falls a Second Time
Prostrate yourself once again.

An unusually large crowd presses behind you. It is hard to breathe. Once again in absolute fatigue and weakness, you fall to the ground. Everything is black. The soldiers whip you again. But for me you drag yourself to your feet once again and continue your journey in love.

The Eighth Station: Jesus Speaks to the Women
Kneel with head bowed to the ground.

Although the law forbids people to show signs of sympathy for prisoners on their way to execution, the women who have seen your fall sob at the sight of you. You, however, tell them to weep for themselves and their children. You want them to be strong in the days of temptation. Teach us to weep for our sins and to do penance to strengthen ourselves for times of testing.

The Ninth Station: Jesus Falls a Third Time
Prostrate yourself a third time.

You collapse once more. For the final time you use every fiber of your being to remember why you are making this journey, and love brings you up for the last few steps. O

Jesus! Help me to love you so much that I will always struggle toward you no matter how difficult the way.

The Tenth Station: Jesus Is Stripped of His Garments
Stand with your hands at your sides, exposing your heart to Jesus.

With cords about your waist, you are dragged to the summit of Calvary, where the soldiers strip you. They do not care if they take pieces of your flesh along with your clothes. You are exposed to all. You possess nothing. You are treated as nothing. But you are everything—our life, our salvation.

The Eleventh Station: Jesus Is Nailed to the Cross
Lie on your back in the form of a cross.

With the crown of thorns still on your head, you are nailed hand and foot to the cross. Then, amid cruel shouts from the mob standing about, your body is lifted up as the cross is raised. Excruciating pains pulse through your legs and back—your whole body. You do not curse or cry out against those who have done this. Instead you forgive your executioners.

The Twelfth Station: Jesus Dies on the Cross
Stand with arms outstretched in the form of a cross.

It wasn't long before most of the crowd drifted away, their thirst for blood and diversion temporarily satisfied. Around noon, a wind blew and darkness came over the land. Fear seized the hearts of all. Soon your heart burst from its agonizing silence as you cried out, "My God, my God, why have you forsaken me?"[5] Then, "I am thirsty." And, about three o'clock, "It is finished."[6]

Last—a loud, final strong cry of perfect faith: "Father, into your hands I commend my spirit."[7]

The Thirteenth Station: Jesus Is Taken Down From the Cross
Kneel with hands cupped, one on top of the other. Then lean

your head to the right, and cradle your head on both hands.

Joseph of Arimathea, a member of the Sanhedrin and a wealthy friend of Nicodemus, who had first come to see you at night, got permission to take your body down from the cross. Already people were drawing strength from your self-gift. Before placing you in the tomb, they put you into your mother's arms. With what sadness she held your broken body; with what gentleness she prepared it for burial; with what perfect love she had walked with you to the end.

The Fourteenth Station: Jesus Is Laid in the Tomb
Lie on your back with your hands crossed over your heart.

Your followers carried your body to a new tomb. By rolling a great stone to block the entrance, they sealed the tomb, which was carved in the side of a rock. Pilate placed a guard there. Nothing human could possibly empower you to walk in this world again. Nothing merely human could break through the bonds of death.

Prayer

Stand, raising your arms in a gesture of thanks and praise; then sign yourself with the cross.

O Jesus, you are God and human. You are my Savior. Help me to walk with you all the days of my life. In the name of the Father and of the Son and of the Holy Spirit. Amen.

Mary: O, my beloved son, well have you meditated on these holy mysteries. And thank you all who have come to pray with us; for when you pray the Stations of the Cross, I can feel your comforting presence with me as the experience of Jesus' crucifixion continues today.

Dominic: To pray with one's body is to pray from one's limitations. This is a prayer that the angels cannot pray. In our humanity, in all of its glorious limitation, there we must praise God!

Mary: Glorify God in your flesh, as the apostle Paul teaches us:

> For while we live, we are always being given up to death for Jesus' sake, so that the life of Jesus may be made visible in our mortal flesh.[8]

Ignatius: As I grew older and my flesh began to weaken, I suffered from much sickness. But as Jesus learned a more perfect obedience from what he suffered,[9] so God taught me a deeper obedience from the pain in my legs and the ulcers in my stomach. I learned to love a Church that was far from perfect. There was much to criticize in the Church of my age. Scandals among the clergy and hypocrisy in Rome are nothing new. In fact, the scandals of your age are relatively tame compared to those of mine.

At one point, I felt I had no choice but to direct my men to pray for the death of the pope, so scandalous was his action. In God's graciousness, our prayer was quickly heard! Truly, all the popes of your century have been pillars of virtue and founts of holy wisdom when compared to some who led the Church in my time.

Friends, as we walk this processional prayer with Christ, we must love those fellow pilgrims whom the Lord puts along our pathways. This is what it means to embrace the cross: to love a blessed and broken Church, to love your graced and grieving families, to love your sacred and sinful cities, to embrace the full expanse of your humanity. Join me in another prayer with the cross.

Ignatius' Cross Meditation

Place a cross or a crucifix on a table, a chair or on the floor in your place of prayer. Stand a few feet away from this symbol, gazing upon it. Recall the words of the Memorial Acclamation: "Lord, by your cross and resurrection, you have set us free. You are the Savior of the world."[10]

Opening Prayer

Standing in place, let us pray:

Gracious God, your Son, Jesus, gave us his command of love. Give us now the strength to live that command, for we have loved too feebly. We have loved too selfishly. Teach us to love as Jesus loves. Empower us in love. Purify our love.

Protect this time of prayer, and help us to enter into those broken places in our own lives that need to be healed by your love. We ask this through Jesus, our crucified Lord, now and forever. Amen!

Take the cross in your hands and position yourself comfortably. Call to mind how this cross came into your life. If the cross you are holding has no special meaning, remember one that does. Savor that memory now. Can you recall any times you have prayed with this cross that stand out as especially meaningful? Take a moment now to ponder these. As you hold this cross, what is the Spirit who speaks beyond your limitations praying in your heart? Where is the crucified Lord present in your life right now?

The Crown of Thorns

John's Gospel recounts that just above Jesus' head was an inscription written at Pilate's command in Hebrew, Latin and Greek: "Jesus of Nazareth, the King of the Jews."[10] *Read that inscription. Gaze upon the head of the King crowned with thorns. Imagine yourself feeling the sharpness of these thorns. How have you, in the agony of your own life, worn that crown of thorns? How have you, with your own sin, pushed the thorns more deeply into the head of Christ by what you have said, thought or done? Place one or two of your fingers upon the crown of Christ as we pray:*

Jesus, you alone can save me. I cannot save myself by my good deeds, my faith or fasting, my piety, prayers or self-punishments. Your love alone saves me. I choose you, Jesus, as my King, my Lord, my God, my Savior; for you have already chosen me as your little one whom you love.

Kiss that crown of suffering as a sign of your willingness to embrace suffering in your own life for the sake of our King.

The Right Hand of Christ

Open your own left hand and look at it. What suffering in your life right now has pierced your hand? Let your wounds be visible to yourself and to our God. Gaze on the right hand of Christ, nailed to the cross. See this hand; it is always open, always ready to heal and strengthen. Extend your left hand to touch the wound in the right hand of Christ.

Jesus, I am wounded; Jesus, be my healing.
Jesus, I am weak; Jesus, be my strength.
Jesus, I am filled with doubt; Jesus, be my assurance.

Kiss the wound you see in your own hand. And kiss the wounded hand Christ stretches out to you in gentle compassion.

The Left Hand of Christ

Open and look at your own right hand. What suffering have you brought to others by your hand? How have you swung the hammer that drove the nail deep into the flesh of Christ? In what ways have you closed your fist, raising it in angry defiance to God?

Look now upon the left hand of Christ, pierced by our sins, forever open, extended in forgiving love to us, giving all into God's hands. Touch the wound in Jesus' left hand.

Jesus, I am unforgiving; Jesus, be my forgiveness.
Jesus, I am unjust; Jesus, be my justice.
Jesus, I am proud; Jesus, be my humility.

The Feet of Christ

Look at your feet. With one hand holding the cross, place your other hand on the feet of the crucified One.

Jesus, you said to Saint Peter, "...[W]hen you were younger, you used to fasten your own belt and to go wherever you wished. But when you grow old, you will stretch out your hands, and someone else will fasten a belt around you and take you where you do not wish to go.... Follow me."[12]

Help me to see where I am reluctant to be led, where I am afraid to follow, what good work I have left undone.

Gaze upon those sacred feet, pierced and bound together by a single nail. Place one hand on or near one of your feet. Place the thumb of the hand that holds the cross on the wound in Christ's feet.

Jesus, I am afraid; Jesus, be my courage.
Jesus, I am lazy; Jesus, be my energy.
Jesus, I am lost; Jesus, be my pathway.

Carry a kiss to your feet with your hand. Kiss the wound in the feet of the crucified One.

The Wounded Side

Gaze on the wound in Christ's side. In John's Gospel, a soldier pierced Jesus' side with a lance. Immediately blood and water flowed out. Touch your hand to the wounded side. From the earliest times, the Church has seen the waters of Baptism and the lifeblood of Eucharist flow endlessly from the pierced heart of Christ.

Let some drop of this holy water, this river of life, fall upon you, where you feel most wounded. Bring your hand to some part of your body where you most need the healing strength of this holy water, this precious blood.

Jesus, I am discouraged; Jesus, be my hope.
Jesus, I am thirsty; Jesus, be my drink.
Jesus, I am hungry; Jesus, be my food.
Jesus, I am captive in my sin; Jesus, be my freedom in
    your grace.
Jesus, I am but your little one: Jesus, be my Lord, my
    God, my Savior, my all.

Kiss your hand and carry that sign of tenderness to the broken parts of yourself. Kiss the wound in the side of Christ. Now hold the cross to the center of your chest near your heart. As we conclude this meditation, join with me, aloud or silently, in an old prayer I raised so often:

Soul of Christ, sanctify me.[13]
Body of Christ, save me.
Blood of Christ, inebriate me.
Water from the side of Christ, wash me.
Passion of Christ, strengthen me.
O Good Jesus, hear me.
Within thy wounds, hide me.
Permit me not to be separated from thee.
From the wicked foe defend me.
At the hour of death call me
and bid me come to thee,

that with all the saints I may praise thee
forever and ever.
Amen.

*With the crucifix in your right hand and facing you, bless
yourself with it, slowly and prayerfully marking yourself
with the Sign of the Cross.*

For Reflection

- Where do I see the disfigured face of Jesus in today's world? How do I minister to him as did Veronica and Simon?

- When I fall, when my life is shattered by divorce, illness, loss of a loved one or termination of a job, am I willing to get up and keep trying to walk with Jesus? Who or what can help me to be faithful to his way?

- Am I willing to let go of the death which is in me and around me? How do I commend my spirit into God's hands as Jesus did?

Closing Prayer

Litany of the Sacred Heart

The Litany of the Sacred Heart holds many beautiful images reminding us of Jesus' love for us. Let us gather, friends, and recite this litany using our whole bodies to pray.

Let us kneel, bowing low to the ground, and beg for the mercy of our loving and compassionate Savior.

Lord, have mercy on us.

Christ, have mercy on us.
Lord, have mercy on us.
Christ, hear us.
Christ, graciously hear us.

Let us stand and raise our arms in praise of our saving God.

God the Father in heaven,
(Response): Have mercy on us.
God the Son, Redeemer of the world,...
God the Holy Spirit,...
Holy Trinity, one God,...

Let us kneel, hands open in front of us, meditating on who Jesus is: perfect Love.

Heart of Jesus, formed by the Holy Spirit in the womb of the Virgin Mother,...
Heart of Jesus, substantially united to the Word of God,...
Heart of Jesus, of infinite majesty,...
Heart of Jesus, tabernacle of the Most High,...
Heart of Jesus, house of God and gate of heaven,...

Still kneeling, let us cross our hands over our hearts and focus on Jesus' love for all.

Heart of Jesus, burning fire of charity,...
Heart of Jesus, abode of justice and love,...
Heart of Jesus, full of loving-kindness,...
Heart of Jesus, treasure house of all virtues,...
Heart of Jesus, most worthy of all praise,...
Heart of Jesus, king and center of all hearts,...

Let us stand straight and stretch out our arms in the shape of the cross.

Heart of Jesus, atonement for our sins,...
Heart of Jesus, overwhelmed with contempt,...
Heart of Jesus, bruised for our offenses,...
Heart of Jesus, obedient unto death,...
Heart of Jesus, pierced with a lance,...

Let us prostrate ourselves before Jesus, who loves us infinitely.

Heart of Jesus, source of all consolation,...
Heart of Jesus, our life and resurrection,...
Heart of Jesus, our peace and reconciliation,...
Heart of Jesus, salvation of those who die in you,...

Let us stand with our heads bowed as we remember the Lamb who was slain.

Lamb of God, who takes away the sins of the world, graciously hear us, O Lord.
Lamb of God, who takes away the sins of the world, have mercy on us.

Still standing with heads bowed, let us cross our hands over our hearts.

Jesus, meek and humble of heart,
make our hearts like unto yours.

Let us bow low from a standing position.

Almighty and eternal God, look upon the heart of your dearly beloved Son, and upon the reparation he offers you on behalf of sinners. Be appeased and grant pardon to those who seek your mercy, in the name of Jesus Christ, your Son, who lives and reigns with you forever and ever.

Let us stand, lifting our faces heavenward in hope-filled assurance.

Amen.

Notes

[1] *I Dream of Peace: Images of War by Children of Former Yugoslavia,* UNICEF (New York: HarperCollins, 1994), p. 74.

[2] Matthew 28:20.

[3] This meditation is inspired by another meditation. See *Prayer Course for Healing Life's Hurts* by Matthew Linn, Dennis Linn and Sheila Fabricant (Mahwah, N.J.: Paulist Press, 1983), p. 77.

[4] John 13:14-15.

[5] Mark 15:34.

[6] John 19:28, 30.

[7] Luke 23:46.

[8] 2 Corinthians 4:11.

[9] See Hebrews 5:8.

[10] *The Roman Missal*, English translation by International Committee on English in the Liturgy, Washington, D.C., 1973.

[11] John 19:19-20.

[12] John 21:18-19.

[13] This is Ignatius' own prayer as found in *The Spiritual Exercises of St. Ignatius: Based on Studies in the Language of the Autograph*, by Louis J. Puhl, S.J. (Chicago: Loyola University Press, 1951), preface.

DAY SIX
Embodying the Resurrection

Coming Together in the Spirit

The Tanda and Duvalty families, while baptized into
the Kingdom, had no real understanding of its light
and happiness. Both families, in different ways, had
grown used to existing in the culture of despair. As
middle-class Americans, they had the necessities of
life. Yet they were bombarded with the bad news of
the world around them: a place where fear, anxiety
and disillusionment hide hope; where billions are
hungry and degraded; where children are daily
exploited. They tried to shield themselves from the
bad news and, in so doing, made it difficult for the
light to break through to their spirits. Nevertheless,
both families were close-knit and survived because
of their mutual love.

Then it happened. The Tandas, driving home from
vacation, were hit by a drunken driver. The youngest
child, Timmy, age six, died instantly. At the same
time, the Duvaltys discovered that their ten-year-old
daughter Jenny needed a new liver and would die if
she did not find a donor soon. The family had no
promise, no protection.

The Tandas, wanting Timmy's life to count for
something, donated his organs. Jenny Duvalty
received Timmy's liver. The Duvaltys shared their
gratitude, their joy in Jenny's being given the chance

for a new life, with the Tandas. The life-giving of the Duvaltys lifted up the Tandas even in their grief.[1]

Defining Our Thematic Context

As Christ has been raised from death, so we hope to be raised one day from the limits of sin and death. Today our mentors reflect on the importance of the anointing of Jesus and upon our sacramental anointing. They share with us some of their Easter joy in the form of a dance prayer.

Opening Prayer

Dear Mother Mary,
pure and perfect conductor of the Light,
on the morning of the Resurrection,
when the sun's rays poured into the empty tomb,
was it like a great flash of light
illuminating, connecting and clarifying
all that you had for so long pondered in your heart?
Or did the light gradually flow into the darkness,
streaming around corners and providing
just what you needed along the way?
Help us, O Mother,
to see that rising with Christ
simply means walking with him
step by step, day by day, year after year,
in service, forgiveness, truth,
humility, peace and love.

O Brother Dominic,
did you love Mary Magdalene

because she had the courage
to set out while it was still dark,
to seek Jesus on the morning after the Sabbath—
to set out to find him
in spite of her weariness, sadness and confusion?
Teach us, Dominic,
when we are in darkness, sin, depression,
sickness, weariness or confusion,
to get up with courage and seek Jesus.

O gentle Father Ignatius,
you let go of armor
and left yourself open to divine wounding
so that you might win the prize of eternal life.
You let go of violence to embrace peace;
you chose service over power
and forgiveness rather than revenge.
In making these passages,
you moved beyond death to life.
Help us to recognize and move away
from death-dealing thoughts, words and actions
to life-giving ones.
Teach us to rise with Jesus forever!

Retreat Session Six

Ignatius: I can see that our retreatants are developing a new suppleness in their prayer. Perhaps all the body postures we have been suggesting are beginning to open them to the power of God's grace.

Dominic: This calls for a celebration!

Mary: Not so soon, Dominic. There will be time for dancing, but we have not yet reached the dawn. We know that daybreak is coming, yet we are still in those wee hours of the morning, the dark hours of the night's long vigil before the birds begin to sing.

Ignatius: You're right, my Lady. These are some of the hardest hours—waiting, wondering, wearying, worrying.

Dominic: A song the Beatles sang about these moments comes to mind. Into the darkness they describe comes Mother Mary, whispering her answer to the angel in Nazareth: "Let it be."

Ignatius: I never knew you were a Beatles fan!

Dominic: Well, as you said yourself, Father Ignatius: *Tantum quantum*: "Use all the things of this earth that help us grow closer to Christ."

Ignatius: Come to think of it, Brother Dominic, that tonsure of yours with the bangs combed straight down does look a bit like an early Beatles hairdo.

Dominic: And with that gleaming globe of yours, I guess you gravitated more toward the Michael Jordan look?

Mary: You two certainly sound like brothers! But, you know, Dominic is right. In the hour of darkness I make my presence known to saints and sinners and songwriters. *Fiat*, "Let it be," was my prayer at the Annunciation. It was also my prayer at the cross. It was my prayer in the dark hours of Holy Saturday.

For then we stumbled in the darkness—stunned, shocked, stripped of our identity. We could not bear for the body of our Beloved to be left, like all the rest, to be food for wild animals and birds of prey. If only he could be buried properly! Thank God for Joseph of Arimathea, who had the courage to request permission from Pilate. And before we closed ourselves behind the doors of the sabbath, we women followed in secret to find the place of the tomb. Then we withdrew and wrapped ourselves in each other's arms to mourn.

We had a task. Sometimes in the midst of mourning there is a task and, if you pour yourself into it, you have a place for all your tears to flow. Ours was a common work, the work of women: to prepare spices and ointments for the body. As our senses were flooded with fragrances, our memories flooded with feelings. All the moments of our loving passed before us, and we shared them—memories pouring together like oils blending, like spices rich and pungent.

Here again was the aroma of myrrh. O, how young I was when my senses first filled with this sweetness! How young my child! Did the wise men know then the meaning of their gift? Could this fragrance have foretold such a future?

Here, the olive oil—olive oil for cooking, for lighting our sabbath lamps and softening our skin, olive oil for our days of joy—the oil of gladness! And we remembered all the anointings in our lives: anointing the heads of our guests as they came to table; anointing the sick, like the Samaritan who gathered the wounded one in his arms and soothed his sores with oil; anointing ourselves even when fasting so as not to draw attention to our practice of penance.

Most importantly, though, we remember the anointing of Jesus before his death.[2] The woman at Bethany must have sensed that death was coming. My soul sings that she anointed him so lavishly! She anointed him like a king, pouring fragrant oil over his head! How rich a perfume—pure nard! The disciples scoffed at her because she loved too much, too publicly; but Jesus rebuked them, saying, "[S]he has anointed my body beforehand for its burial."[3] She broke the alabaster jar to release the fragrance. Jesus' spirit, too, was released when that body was broken.

In his last days, my son withdrew to the Mount of Olives and rested in the olive groves. He struggled at Gethsemane and cried out in the garden whose name means "oil press." Soon afterwards, the life of my son was pressed out of him. And now we poured the oil pressed from olives—sacred oil—to bless him and bury him. As we prayed and cried and prepared, all these memories and images wafted through our midst. Soon, our ritual of remembering was complete.

And then it was time for us to choose just a few of us to go to the tomb. These three, yes, let them go. I held my son one last time, but they did not. Let them go with loving hands. At daybreak, let them go bearing fragrances to soften and sweeten the blows of death—to touch and reverence and bid farewell. Yes, we thought, let us rest now until the night is done. And in the morning, let there be light.

And in the morning he came to the women! Easter! Christ rose through the gaping wounds of our mourning—the ripped-out places, the red-rubbed faces, the raw and wretched—and left in each place new life! The appointed morning—yes, mourning into dancing—had come!

Dominic: Mother, let me remind our pilgrims how John recounts this scene in his Gospel. When Mary Magdalene arrived at the place where Jesus was buried, she saw the stone rolled away from an empty tomb and wandered about, weeping disconsolately. She could not discern Christ through her tear-weary eyes. Instead she thought it was the gardener who kindly asked her, "Woman, why are you weeping? Whom are you looking for?"... [Unable to contain her grief, Mary poured forth her heart.] "Sir, if you have carried him away, tell me where you have laid him, and I will take him away."[4]

At that moment, Jesus called her by name. "Mary!" What a change took place in her heart when she heard her beloved call her name! Bursting with joy, she rushed forward to embrace him! But Jesus called her to a new depth of love. He called her to witness to his triumph over death—not by clinging to him, but by telling the others.

How I love Mary Magdalene! How often I entrusted my sisters to her in prayer! In her, friends, as in all the saints, the transforming power of the resurrected Christ shines forth brilliantly.

Ignatius: Some misinterpret Jesus' action and think Jesus is somehow rejecting Magdalene. Far from rejecting her, he is commissioning her. Her love for him must now grow and stretch into a whole new dimension.

Dominic: Parents, for example, beget children and those children grow up and have sons and daughters of their own. As the family circle widens, so do problems and concerns as well as joy and other good gifts. More and more courage is called forth from the original parents— now grandparents—as the years progress. They cannot cling to each other and ignore the needs of succeeding generations. They cannot cling to family and ignore those among whom their family grows. They cannot cling to their youthful strength and health or to status in the community or at work. No, love that clings really isn't love. Love by its nature stretches and stretches, gives thanks for what is good, rejoices in the moment and opens itself to embrace the next.

Mary: My son reaches out to embrace us all. Even now I see him in his robe of resurrection. Do you see him—gleaming, brilliant, white as snow? His light floods the face of the earth—the dawn of a new creation. But look closely: You can also see his wounds. They did not disappear in his rising; they were transformed, for these wounds brought him to this new place and ushered in the redemption. His blood has made us pure! We can reach out to touch his wounds now.

Ignatius: Yes, Mother. We need to know that God is with us. No one is helped by some distant god living in a remote corner of the universe. The wounds of the risen Christ remind us that, even in his glory, Christ Jesus remains united to his suffering body on earth.

The twelve-step programs that have spread throughout the world are gatherings of people who are willing to break the code of silence. They courageously share the pain of their lives with one another. In other words, they allow one another to touch their woundedness. And the infected wounds in their psyches are transformed into holy, sacred wounds. The grace of the Resurrection is at work here. The transforming power of the Holy Spirit is being released.

Dominic: And blessed are we who have not seen, yet believe. We are anointed with Christ's love, and there is no stronger power in the universe.

Mary: Yes, Dominic, I'm so glad you describe Christ's love as an anointing. For Christ's love pours out on us like rich oil. And as you know, on the morning of Resurrection, when the women went to the tomb to anoint Jesus' body, they discovered that Jesus had no need of the fragrances and oil we had prepared. His body was made new, glorified, streaming with light. We were the ones who needed to be healed and made whole. We needed to learn how to believe, to be called through woundedness into new life. So Jesus left the oil of anointing for us!

Anointing is a powerful ritual action that is used sacramentally by the ordained in many Christian Churches. But all Christians by virtue of their Baptism may bless and pray with oil as a rich symbol of Christ's transforming Spirit. When we are anointed in Christ's name, we are touched by Christ's healing love. We are called through death into new life. And we are commissioned to bear the Good News to all the world.

So, my friends, the time has come. Dominic, Ignatius and I ask you to pass with Christ and with us through the cross into the Resurrection. Now is the time for the Holy Spirit to touch whatever wounds you carry with healing power. As you bless yourself with holy oil, may you come to know your place in the priesthood of the people, baptized in the blood of the Lamb and made whiter than snow. Let me lead you.

Mary's Anointing Meditation

For this meditation you will need some oil and a small bowl. Since biblical times, Jews and Christians alike have most commonly used olive oil for anointing. You may use olive oil or some other type of plant oil. Massage oils, many of which are a blend of healing ingredients, would be appropriate, as would perfumed oil. You may want to play some reflective music and dim the lights.

Seat yourself comfortably and pour a small bit of oil

*into your bowl. Cradle the bowl in your hands, and begin
your meditation with a breathing exercise. Fill your lungs
slowly and deeply, breathing in the fragrance of your oil.
Allow its sweetness to fill your being. In the early Church,
scented oil reminded Christians of the sweetness of life in
Christ. Saint Paul called Christians the aroma of Christ.
Breathe again and pray that you, like your ancestors in the
faith, may become the perfume of Christ. Then bless your
oil, consecrating it as a symbol of God's love.*

Stretch out your hands over the bowl and pray:

Creator God, we give you thanks. You brought forth
from the earth the vegetation and the fruit-bearing
trees from which we have the gift of this oil. By your
command, Moses anointed Aaron as priest and
Samuel anointed David as king. In the ancient
tradition, entire flasks of oil were poured over their
heads, showering your servants with strength,
holiness and wisdom.

Loving God, we give you thanks. By the Spirit
you anointed your Son as priest, prophet and king.
You sent the woman of Bethany to anoint Jesus
before his death, preparing him for the Resurrection.

Sanctifying God, we give you thanks, for you
have provided us with oil for healing. In your Spirit,
Jesus sent out the Twelve to preach repentance, to
anoint the sick with oil and cure them. And so we
ask you to bless this oil today. As you have done
throughout the ages, pour forth your strength and
your grace into this oil and into all who are anointed
with it. Help us to deepen our appreciation for this
holy symbol that we may live more fully our
consecration to you. This we ask in Jesus' name.
Amen.

*Look at your hands. What work do they do? Whom have
they touched? Hold in your hands your longing for*

God's transforming grace.

Reach out to Christ, the Anointed One. Ask him to touch your hands. (Pause here to pray.)

Dip your fingers into the oil. Feel its texture on your fingers. One by one, mark your palms with the cross of Christ. Remember that the risen Christ still bears the wounds of the cross. As you mark your palms, imagine that Jesus himself is touching your wounds, marking your palms with his love. He asks you to surrender yourself into his care and open yourself to live in the light of his Resurrection.

Slowly rub your hands together, massaging the oil deep into your hands. As you continue to work the richness into your skin, let God's love for you seep into your hands. May this holy oil soothe you and soften your rough edges. May it clear away all fear and fault. May your hands open to receive the gifts the Lord has in waiting for you, and may you recognize him in the breaking of the bread.

Open your hands. May this holy oil strengthen you to give of yourself, to touch those in need, and to give and receive the greeting of peace throughout your days. And may your hands be consecrated as healing hands that all their labors may be labors of love.

Rest your hands on top of each other, palms open. Imagine Jesus holding your hands in his. Let him speak to you in love. Pause here and pray.

The Roman Catholic Rite of Baptism *includes two anointings. First is the anointing with the Oil of Catechumens to strengthen you with the power of Christ and prepare you for the challenge of Christian living. To renew the power of this great blessing, I now invite you to anoint your heart. You may need to loosen your clothes a bit so that you can reach the center of your chest.*

Breathe deeply, filling your lungs. Is your heart heavy or hopeful, fearful or hurt? Is your heart angry or anxious?

Hold in your heart the challenge you must face in your Christian journey. Now dip your fingers in the oil and mark a cross at the center of your chest. Gently rub the oil into your skin, and feel it penetrating to your heart. Continue massaging your chest or let your hand rest on your heart as we pray:

Come, Holy Spirit, flame of love.
When our hearts are broken, console us.
When our hearts are hardened, soften them.
When our hearts are frozen, burn within us.

Let your hand rest on your heart now. Feel your heart beating. Feel your heart on fire with the Spirit that Jesus sends. Imagine that Jesus is before you now, placing his hand on your hand as you touch your heart. With your free hand, reach out to touch his Sacred Heart. Feel the love of his heart reaching out to you. Pause and pray.

The second anointing associated with Baptism is a blessing on the crown of your head so that you might come to know your dignity in Christ. Remember also the spiritual energy that encircles the head of saints and holy ones, often pictured in the form of a halo. Pray that you, too, may wear such a crown.

Take a small bit of oil, and mark the top of your head with the cross of Christ. Lift your hands above your head and call down the Spirit. Hear God's voice saying to you as to Jesus at his Baptism, "This is my beloved child in whom I am well pleased."

Open your arms out to your sides till they are outstretched in prayer. Let us pray:

As Christ was anointed priest, prophet and king, so may you live in the royal priesthood of your baptismal calling. When you come to Eucharist as a member of Christ's Body, may you rejoice with the community of believers and recognize Jesus in the breaking of the bread.

Lower your hands. Recall the anointing of your forehead at Confirmation, when the Holy Spirit strengthened and sealed your commitment to Christ. Take a bit of oil and sign your forehead with a cross. Then gently rub the oil into your brow. Slowly massage away your doubts, your fears and your cares—whatever worry or tension you carry. Be sealed with the gift of the Holy Spirit. May your mind be filled with wisdom and understanding, right judgment and courage, knowledge and reverence, wonder and awe.

For our final anointing, I invite you to choose an area of your body that you feel is in need of special blessing— perhaps your feet, your knees, your belly. In the early Church, sometimes the entire body of those in need was anointed, but I'll ask you to just choose one part of yourself, the place where you feel a special need for grace or healing. For what does this part of yourself cry out: strength, love, tenderness, courage?

Take a bit of oil and sign this area of yourself with a cross; then gently rub the oil into your skin.

Through this anointing, may the Lord in his soothing love and healing mercy help you with the grace of the Holy Spirit. May the Lord who frees you from sin save you and raise you up. Amen.[5]

Bow your head and pray for God's blessing.

May our God, Creator, Redeemer and Sanctifier consecrate your body that you may know yourself a member of God's chosen race, royal priesthood, holy people. From this anointing, may you know that the Spirit of the Lord God is upon you. For the Holy One has anointed you. God sends you to bring good news to the poor, to bind up hearts that are broken, to proclaim liberty to captives, to comfort those who mourn and to give them the oil of gladness.[6]

Now live in the light of the Resurrection. Marked by the oil of gladness, may you go! Amen!

Ignatius: Is it time to dance now, Mary?

Mary: Yes, Ignatius, it's time to dance!

Dominic: I've been waiting for this. Are you ready, Ignatius?

Ignatius: I'm not so sure. I've become accustomed to the prayer postures, but I haven't been practicing my pirouettes!

Mary: Christ calls us into the liberating light of the Resurrection; but for those who watch from safe shadows, the people out there dancing in the light can seem rather foolish!

Ignatius: That reminds me of the story of the women who returned from the tomb bright and beaming and tripping over themselves to share with the Eleven the news of the risen Lord.

Dominic: That's right; and to the men, the women's story seemed absolute nonsense. There was no way on earth they were going to let go of their grieving for a story like that.

Mary: Yes, in some ways we cling to our own sorrow, and often that boils down to a fear of appearing foolish. In my day, dancing was a part of life, the most natural way of celebrating. Remember the wedding at Cana? After Jesus changed the water to wine, you should have seen the dancing—Jesus and all his disciples included!

Ignatius: I don't think we've ever heard that part of the story. But it just goes to show, Mary, you were lucky. To some people today, dance is a language they've never learned to speak.

Mary: I know, Ignatius. And for those who are self-conscious, dancing is by no means easy.

Ignatius: Take, for example, that first Easter morning when the disciples began to let the reality of the Resurrection penetrate the barriers they had erected. After scoffing at the women, they finally began to listen when testimony came from men! First was Jesus' appearance to Simon and the reports of the two on the road to Emmaus. Then Jesus appeared to the Eleven.

Dominic: Yes, and they were shocked; they were alarmed and frightened. They thought they were seeing a ghost.

Ignatius: And when they finally realized it was Jesus, their joy was so great that they just stood there dumbfounded.

Mary: That's how I felt when the angel first appeared to me: dumbfounded!

Ignatius: But how does one move from dumbfounded to delighted?

Mary: Well, Jesus helps a lot. Do you remember what he said to them?

Ignatius: "Peace be with you."

Dominic: Ah, yes, "Peace be with you." And the disciples were filled with joy. Their hearts melted; their eyes shone with new possibilities.

Mary: Then Jesus breathed into them the Holy Spirit. And the Spirit is what empowers and inspires and moves us all.

Ignatius: Moves us to dancing?

Mary: Well, let's start with something simple, Ignatius—a gesture dance.

Mary's Prayer for Peace

First, it would be of great help for you to find a copy of the music for this simple and beautiful song, "Prayer for Peace," by David Haas,[7] but you may prefer just to recite the words prayerfully. The text of the song is based on an ancient Navajo prayer. The Native Americans sensed God's peaceful goodness in all of creation. The disciples received God's special gift of peace from the risen Christ. Today, if we take time to breathe in the gift of nature, if we take time to breathe in the gift of Christ's Holy Spirit, we too can be filled with peace. When we know peace, we can share this gift with the world. Let us pray, and let us dance.

(Starting position)   Peace before us,   Peace behind us,

(back)

Peace   under   under   within us.   Peace   over us.
          our feet.   our feet.

Let all around us be peace.

Peace before us.

With palms facing the earth, lift your arms slightly until they hover at your sides like eagle's wings. Then, draw your arms forward till your hands cross at the wrist in front of you. Visualize a circle of safety and peace that our God is creating before you now and for all your days to come.

Peace behind us.

Open your arms outward. Let them pass by your sides until your arms reach behind you, hands gently touching in back. Imagine God's love and comfort circling behind you, bringing peace even to your past.

Peace under our feet.

On "peace," circle your arms to the front again. This time let your hands come next to each other and turn your palms up. On "under our feet," bend your knees and crouch down so that your hands gesture to the earth. Pray that the earth below our feet may be blessed, and that you may plant your feet in Christ's peace and stand in his grace.

Peace within us, peace over us.

From your low position by the earth, point your fingers down as if you were putting your hands into the wellspring of Christ's peace. Then draw your fingers up and spread them out gently, as if water were flowing through them. Do this gesture four times: at knee level, at your waist, at your chest, over your head. Imagine you are drawing living water up from the earth. It rises through your center, bubbles up to your chest and spills out over all. Open your arms out wide on this last gesture, overflowing with Christ's gift of peace.

Let all around us be peace.

Now offer peace to the world. Let your hands form a bowl near your heart. Extend your arms forward; then, spread

*them out wide and open, giving Christ's gift to the world.
As you do this, turn around in place and offer the peace of
Christ to those who pray with you, and to all of God's great
family.*

*This song has six verses. Five meditate on different
words:* peace, love, light, Christ, alleluia; *a concluding
verse returns to* peace. *Repeat the same set of gestures on
each verse, except for the fifth (alleluia) verse. There simply
stand in place and sway, palms open in prayer. Or join
hands with those praying with you as one Body in Christ.
There's a little time for swaying between verses, as well.*

*Now the dance is yours! May the peace of Christ be
with you always: before you, behind you, within you,
among you. Amen.*

For Reflection

- How do I seize the power of the resurrected Christ
  and allow that power to find ways to work in me—to
  heal, to feed, to offer hope to my brothers and sisters?

- Am I more afraid of my own physical death than of
  spiritual death? If so, why is this true? In what ways
  will I protect myself from choosing spiritual death?

- How do I affirm the God of life for those who need to
  rise from depression, skepticism or lack of faith?

Closing Prayer

In the power of God's all-pervading peace, let us take
a moment, good friends, to conclude our day of prayer by
praising the glory of the Trinity.

As you breathe in deeply, clench your fists tightly and cross
your arms over your chest. Remember the pain that pulsed
through you as you owned your rage, selfishness, isolation,
greed, pride, fear and lack of forgiveness—all the ways sin
has held you captive in your self-carved tomb.

Then, bowing your head, ask Jesus to take these dark
things one by one into the tomb with him. Feel yourself
surrendering them to the Holy Trinity as you exhale slowly.

Glory be to the Father,...

Breathe deeply. And as you exhale, uncross one of your
arms and lower it to your side. Keep your fist clenched, but
allow yourself to feel some of the joy that comes in praising
God. Picture yourself bathed in the warm, golden light of
love.

And to the Son,...

Take another deep breath and, as you exhale, uncross your
other arm. Your heart is now uncovered. Jesus stands before
you. See his Sacred Heart ablaze with love, his heart aglow
in the center of his chest. Imagine the gentle strength of his
love flowing into your heart. Imagine Jesus placing his
hand on your heart. Breathe deeply of this love. Take in his
strength. Exhale the darkness.

And to the Holy...

Breathe deeply and slowly as you open one fist. Let go of
what you need to release.

...Spirit,...

Breathe again and open the other fist. Receive what you
need to receive.

As it was in the beginning,...

Keep your eyes closed. Raise your head slightly so that your
gaze is straight ahead. Look into the eyes of Jesus, who was
with the Father and the Spirit in the beginning, the One

who knows you—has known you from the beginning—and who loves you.

Is now,...

Stretch your arms forward to Jesus. Surrender to him your cares and worries, fears and failures. Receive his strength, his trust, his mercy.

And ever shall be,...

Lift your face to the sky. Look into the future of your life with hope, with confident assurance in the One who made you, redeemed you and will forever sustain you.

World without end.

Lift your arms to the heavens. Reach to receive the divine embrace. Let your spirit be raised high in praise of the One who loves you beyond all telling. Again feel the warmth of God's presence flowing over you, covering you like a waterfall of love.

Amen!

Open your eyes to this truth. Open your heart to this love. Open your soul to this blessing.

Amen.

Lower your gaze in humble surrender. Bring your palms together, fingers pointing to the sky. Allow this love to continue to warm you and empower you and show you how to witness to the risen Jesus. As you share this truth with others, you will recognize both love and joy deepening within you. This is knowing the power of the risen Christ!

Notes

[1] Based on a true incident.

[2] See Matthew 26:6-13; Mark 14:3-9; John 12:1-11.

[3] Mark 14:8b.

[4] John 20:15.

[5] Adapted from the *Rite of Anointing of the Sick* (International Commission on English in the Liturgy, Washington, D.C., 1982).

[6] See Isaiah 61:1.

[7] A recording of David Haas' song "Prayer for Peace" can be found in the collection *As Water to the Thirsty*, copyright ©1987, published by GIA Publications, Inc. (7404 S. Mason Ave., Chicago, IL 60638). The recorded song, along with a full description of gestures, is also available from St. Anthony Messenger Press in the collection *Full Body Blessing: Praying With Movement* by Betsey Beckman, Michael Sparough, S.J., and Bobby Fisher (1615 Republic St., Cincinnati, OH 45210).

DAY SEVEN
Dancing in Divine Love

Coming Together in the Spirit

A young disciple decided to do an apprenticeship under a master spiritual teacher. After many months of difficult spiritual practices, the young disciple complained that no spiritual benefit was forthcoming.

"Will these prayers and meditations bring me closer to God?" the young disciple blurted out impatiently one day.

"Possibly," spoke the master, "but not necessarily. They will have as little impact on your drawing closer to God as you will have in making the sun rise tomorrow morning."

The disciple was confused and angry. "Then what good is all this rigorous spiritual discipline?"

The master only smiled. "To make sure that you're not asleep when the sun does rise."[1]

Defining Our Thematic Context

The final movement of this retreat is a call to celebrate the wonder of God's Spirit moving within us and through us and calling us beyond ourselves. Our mentors teach us to surrender ourselves to divine love and to offer ourselves as servants to the community, the Body of

Christ. With the joy of Jesus in our hearts, we are called to share with others the love that has been so freely given to us.

Opening Prayer

Mother Mary, brother Dominic, dear Ignatius,
You know the gift of grace in all its gentleness.
Teach me to open my eyes and hands and heart
to its wonder.
Bring me into the light of our Lord.
For grace comes unexpected, unseen—
But when I open my eyes,
grace is everywhere—
rubbing against my cheek,
falling in tears,
filling each breath,
unfolding in flowers.

I have opened my heart to you, God,
and you have given me more
than I ever imagined,
hands overflowing with the fullness of life.
Now lead me, Lord,
ever more into your loving presence.
I say yes, O Lord,
to your leading.
Send me forth afire
and bring me home made new,
full of the freshness of things.

May I open my eyes always
to the goodness of your grace
bringing me to the source of my own soul,
rooting me deep
in the soil of you.

Retreat Session Seven

Dominic: And so we have come to our seventh day.

Ignatius: Ah, yes. Genesis tells us that on the seventh day God rested. I can easily imagine the Creator sitting back, so to speak—putting the divine feet up and enjoying all that has been made.

Mary: Yes, dear brother, that's one way of picturing it. But imagine God giving birth to all of creation. The labors of childbirth are no easy thing! After six days of giving birth, God must have been exhausted!

Ignatius: All these years I've counseled people to use their imagination to enter into the biblical stories, I've never imagined God as a *woman* in the process of creation.

Mary: Well, my dear son, while you've been learning to dance, I suspect your imagination exercises have been rubbing off on me! It goes to show that mothers can always be open to learning from their children.

Dominic: I don't know about you two, but I think *I'm* ready for a rest.

Ignatius: It must be all those prayer calisthenics you've been having us do. "Now lie prostrate, now kneel, now arch heavenward." Who needs the gym when Dominic is around?

Mary: We have shared so much, haven't we? And our retreatant friends have walked so boldly with us.

Ignatius: It is not that we have attempted to step out into unexplored territory. This trek has been of another sort. We have journeyed with you, fellow retreatants, down paths that we have walked before, but that have been forgotten by many. These paths are tested and true, and yet they are all too often thought suspect or strange.

Dominic: To search for God, to long for God, to seek God before all else is a bold enterprise. This is not a voyage for the fainthearted!

Ignatius: Like the travelers on the road to Emmaus, all of our hearts have burned within us as we have shared the mysteries of Christ's enduring Spirit.

Mary: And our love for you, which has always been so strong in heaven, now has flesh and bones on it, for we have danced together! And now we rejoice in the presence of the risen Lord. We have labored hard these past six days, and yet, as Jesus told us: "When a woman is in labor, she has pain, because her hour has come. But when her child is born, she no longer remembers the anguish because of the joy of having brought a human being into the world."[2]

Christ's labors are complete, and we have all been brought to new birth. No one can take our joy from us.

Dominic: Remember the Easter antiphon:

> This is the day that the Lord has made;
> let us rejoice and be glad in it.

Mary: Yes, Dominic. That reminds me of what we experienced in the wonderful aftermath of Easter. For forty days we lived with Jesus in our midst—walking with us to Emmaus, eating fish with us, sharing his peace, filling us with a totally new sense of his love. We were constantly in a state of prayer—not of petition or longing, but the simple prayer of hearts filled to overflowing with love. We sang together, we danced on the beach at the shore of Tiberias, we leaned into each other's love. And Jesus told us to remain in Jerusalem, and to wait there together for the outpouring of the Spirit.

This was the beginning of our new-fledged community. You see, Jesus was with us in a new way. No longer did we look to him to make our day-to-day decisions. All of us began to recognize the unique gifts that we brought to the community and we came forward to share what we had to offer, men and women alike.

We were a large group, a hundred and twenty of us in all. As the Torah instructed, we counted off the days of the seven weeks after Passover that led to our next celebration, *Shavuot*, or "Feast of Weeks." You know this feast by its Greek name—*Pentecost*, "the fiftieth day."

On the fortieth day, we gathered with Jesus on the Mount of Olives. Some of the disciples, filled with exuberance, were eager to know if the time had come for Jesus to restore the kingdom to Israel. When Jesus answered us, we did not understand what he meant—that we were to receive power from the Holy Spirit. Up to this point, the power had rested in Jesus, and we simply reflected holy light. How were we to be imbued with power? How were we to be his witnesses to the ends of the earth?

As we were standing there grappling with his words, suddenly the sky opened. Above us radiated a brilliant light and Jesus was swallowed up by the heavens and covered with the cloud of God—gone.

He was gone! We made our way back to the Upper Room, where we had been staying, and we devoted ourselves to prayer. The hours passed slowly, ten days of counting, counting till we came to the fiftieth day, and finally our fasting ended! Like all the other Jews in the city, we feasted on the stories of our beloved Torah. Here we recounted how God had carried the Israelites out of Egypt on eagles' wings,[3] and how in the desert God called his people to prepare for the covenant. On the third day at Mt. Sinai, there were peals of thunder and lightning flashes, a dense cloud and blaring trumpet blast. Then Yahweh descended on the mountain in the form of fire. Fire! The first covenant came in fire!

As we prayed so fervently, we felt as if *we* were on the mountaintop with Moses. There, God told the Israelites, "...[Y]ou shall be for me a priestly kingdom and a holy nation."[4] And so we became, a kingdom of priests trembling at the thunder, climbing through dense clouds, waiting for the fire. And suddenly, the mountaintop faded, and in our midst we heard what sounded like a powerful wind. It filled the entire house. It shook us to our bones. And then there appeared to us—fire!

At first blazing in a dazzling ball, it separated and came to each of us. It enflamed our hearts; it loosed our tongues! We surrendered and on eagles' wings we soared. Out on the streets were the pilgrims, all the Jews from foreign lands. Ablaze, we could not stop ourselves; we sent out sparks to the earth, sparks of new life. And when we spoke of our beloved Lord, all our fear faded, for it was not we who were speaking, but the Spirit spoke through us. And people listened and heard and believed. We were like Moses, the skin on our faces radiant with light.[5] We were drunk with the love of our Lord.

O my children, it is so good to tell you this story of wonder. For just as God's Spirit had once poured through me to bring Jesus to birth, so on the day of Pentecost God's Spirit poured out on all of us and we witnessed a new birth. That day I became more than mother to my son. I became mother of a whole new Church.

This is the same Spirit God pours out on you. You, too, are instruments of the Kingdom. Do you feel the strength of God's power buoying you up, filling your hearts and sending you forth?

Dominic: Dear Mother Mary, your words are so inspiring. How can we recapture the power of your story in our lives? How can we allow the Spirit to move so potently through us?

Mary: Once again, Dominic, it is time to pray. And by now, our pilgrim friends know the power of praying with their whole beings, body and soul!

Dominic: Let us pray to become instruments of God's empowering Spirit, as you are, Mother. May we, too, become reeds of God.

Mary: My friends, we invite you to an embodied invocation of the Holy Spirit.

Ignatius: As we pray together, let us breathe deeply, allowing God's great Spirit to move in our inmost being.

'Come Holy Spirit'

An Invocation

Dominic: O most magnificent Creator, before the dawn of creation there was darkness over the deep and your Spirit hovered over the waters. When you fashioned from clay the very first humans, you blew into their nostrils the breath of your life.[6]

Ignatius: O powerful Source of our being, when Ezekiel was in the land of the dry bones, he called on you to come from the four winds, and your Spirit blew new breath into the flesh of lifeless bones.[7]

Mary: O liberating Lord, when your Spirit came to us on Pentecost, the room was rocked by the wind of your wisdom, and you set our hearts on fire with new life. We thank you for the gift of your Spirit, renewed in us with every breath of our being.

All: O Holy Spirit, you call us constantly to renewal. And you call us constantly to renew the world with your love. Be with us now as we invoke your grace.

Mary: Friends, to begin our movement prayer, we invite you to center yourself in a circle of God's love. Turn to your left and walk clockwise around the rim of a circle. Imagine that this ring of safety is filled with the fire of Christ's love, and step into its center to begin your prayer.

Dominic: Or simply stand and bow silently to the four directions, your bows making a cross of Christ's love.

Ignatius: Or stand with one hand on your heart and the other hand extended out in blessing. Then turn slowly around in a circle, imagining God's loving protection surrounding you.

Mary: However you choose to begin, when you are ready, stand in the center of your circle. Just as our Jewish ancestors blessed the four directions on the harvest Feast of Booths, *Sukkot*, I invite you now to do the same, sending God's Spirit to the four corners of the earth. Begin by facing the east, toward the dawn of a new creation, toward the light of the Resurrection, and pray:

Mary's Movement Prayer

'Come, Holy Spirit'

Come Holy Spirit, fill the hearts of your faithful...
Lift your face and arms to heaven and pray for the gift of the Holy Spirit. Breathe deeply and open your heart to receive God's transforming love.

...and kindle in us the fire of your love...
Lower your hands to your heart, receiving the fire of God's love, letting it burn in the center of your being.

Send forth your Spirit, and we shall be recreated...
Extend your hands out in blessing, sending God's Spirit to the ends of the earth. Then bring your hands to your heart again, inviting the Spirit you have sent forth to return bearing new gifts.

...and you shall renew the face of the earth.
Lower your arms and bow to the great God who transforms not only us but also our entire earth, bringing grace to all God's creatures and all the elements of creation.

Come, Holy Spirit...
Now turn to the south, and repeat your prayer. Send forth God's renewing Spirit and see God's grace reaching far beyond the earth's equator to all the developing lands and peoples who dwell where summer is winter and winter is summer.

Then turn to the west, and pray again to the land of the setting sun, to the peoples and places where night is morning and morning is night, beyond the horizon to the ends of the earth. Finally, turn toward the north, and send God's fiery love to melt even the coldest hearts, bringing light to all the regions above. Amen!

Mary: Dear retreatants, I hope this prayer brings you a sense of joy and exhilaration in sharing the gift of God's Spirit with all the earth.

Ignatius: Holy Mother, as we pray for Christ's Spirit to dance within us and to carry us beyond our own small concerns, I am reminded of a beautiful prayer written by my sister in faith, Teresa of Avila. She and I were fed by one Spirit, for we walked the earth during the same years.

Mary: Please share with us her prayer, Ignatius.

Ignatius: Certainly. And perhaps I will add some simple gestures to help us pray.

Dominic: Imagine that! Ignatius is leading us in gestures!

Ignatius: When the Spirit leads, I must follow! Here we go.

Christ's Body[8]

Christ has no body now on earth but yours.
  Cross your arms over your chest.

Yours are the only hands with which he can do his work.
  Open your hands before you.

Yours are the only feet with which he can go about the world.
  Touch your feet.

Yours are the only eyes through which his compassion...

Cover your eyes with your hands.

...can shine forth upon a troubled world.
Open your eyes, and open your hands.

Christ has no body on earth now but yours.
Again, cross your arms over your chest.

Mary: How I wish that more of my children would come together in dances of praise and thanksgiving. Our God made us creatures of flesh and blood; male and female God created us. Let us delight in our bodies and give God praise as did Miriam, David and the holy saints of old.

Ignatius: As you say, Mother, we are to glorify God in our flesh! After all, we were not created as angels.

Mary: Embracing the beauty of our bodies in prayerful movement is an act of confidence in the Resurrection. The Spirit raised Jesus body and soul from the grave. Likewise, through his gift of love the Spirit raised me, "assumed" me body and soul to be with my son. All of you who are faithful to him will one day taste in your flesh the fruit of this victory over sin and death.

Ignatius: Mother, remember how I kept an all-night vigil, standing and kneeling before a statue of the Black Madonna at Montserrat, Spain? At the end of my prayer I offered you my sword as a symbol of consecrating myself to you.

Mary: Yes, my son, I remember it well.

Dominic: Ignatius, I too dedicated myself to Mary. To this day, many Dominican communities follow this tradition and place themselves in Mary's care. Let me share with you one of my favorite prayers to the Queen of Heaven, a prayer of dedication and surrender.

Ignatius: Dominic, our response to God's love is truly meant to be an act of surrender. When we surrender to Mary, we surrender to the will of her divine son. You desire to share with us a prayer to Mary; let me join you and share the prayer that welled up in me in gratitude to her son.

Dominic: As you say, Ignatius. Our communities have fought each other over theology. Let us pray together in the Spirit of all unity. Dear friends, pray with us these prayers of surrender. Let us kneel before our Queen.

Ignatius: And King.

Dominic: With our hands open and empty before us, let us offer ourselves to their loving service.

Dominic's and Ignatius' Prayer of Surrender [9]

Dominic: My Queen, my Mother,
I give myself entirely to you;

Ignatius: Take, Lord, and receive all my liberty,
my memory, understanding, and my entire will.
All that I have and possess.

Dominic: And to show my devotion to you,
I consecrate to you my eyes, my ears,
my mouth, my hands, my heart,
my whole being without reserve.

Ignatius: You have given all to me,
To you, O Lord,
I return it.
All is yours,
Use it only according to your will.

Dominic: Wherefore, good Mother, since I am yours,
keep me, guard me, as your own.

Ignatius: Give me only your love and your grace,
with these I am rich enough
and desire nothing more.

Dominic: Amen.

Ignatius: Amen!

Mary: Thank you, dear sons, and loyal retreatants.

Ignatius: Offering all that we think, say, or do to God at the beginning of the day is a beautiful way to be mindful of consecrating our daily lives to God.

Dominic: Another way is to take time at the end of the day to pray. Dear friends, as we draw near to the end of our retreat together, I would like to invite you to pray at the end of the day by reflecting with me on the corporal works of mercy. Use this as a meditation on your call to be merciful, and also as a way of asking if you have found ways to act mercifully during your day.

As I name each specific work that God asks us to perform, I will suggest a posture to help embody our prayer. To help focus your prayer, you may want to put before you a crucifix, perhaps one with the glorified Christ.

The Corporal Works of Mercy [10]

As we pray, let us remember that Christ calls us all:

To feed the hungry.

*Stand before the cross of Christ with your hands cupped
and stretched out in front of you as if you are begging for
food. If you are hungry, place your hand where you feel that
hunger. For example, place one hand over your stomach if
you are craving physical food, over your heart if you are
hungry for companionship. Recognize your hunger so that
you will be better prepared to satisfy the hunger of others.*

To give drink to the thirsty.

*Standing before your Redeemer, place both your hands on
your throat and give thanks for all the beverages you have
taken in this day. Be mindful of how many thirst-quenchers
are available to you every day. Call to mind some thirsts
you may have which liquids cannot quench. What are these
thirsts? Who around you is thirsty? How can you offer
them life-giving water?*

To clothe the naked.

*Move to your closet bodily or in your imagination. Raise
your hands in praise of God who has made it possible for
you to have something appropriate to wear. Do you have
many clothes to give to those who have none? With your
hands on your heart, close your eyes and pray for those who
suffer because they have nothing to wear, nothing to put on
for reasonable comfort, reasonable confidence, reasonable
respect.*

To visit and ransom captives.

*Lie flat on your back beneath the cross. Put your arms at
your sides and pretend you cannot lift them from the
ground. Call to mind the inmates who wait on death row.
Think of those who are captive in their beds because of*

illness, captive in their countries because of powerlessness,
captive to their addictions. Is there someone you could
visit? Pray for all those who have not experienced the
freeing power of mercy and forgiveness.

To give shelter to the homeless.

Sit with your knees pulled up. Bend your head to rest on
your knees. Cover your head with your hands. Think of how
you are sheltered and cared for by God. Reflect on the home
in which you live. Then rise slowly from that position and
open your arms in a gesture of welcoming love to those who
have nowhere to turn for a safe place to live. How will you
minister to the homeless?

To visit the sick.

In a standing position, stretch out your arms in the shape of
a cross. Think of those with frail and broken bodies, those
with fever and pain, those who groan and sigh, those who
are cut off from others. Sickness is a cross. How can you
help someone else to carry it by making the burden lighter?

To bury the dead.

Prostrate yourself before the cross. Remember how all of us
must pass through the moment of death in order to come to
fullness of life. Think of someone—not necessarily someone
you know—now dying. Beg Jesus to remind that person of
his love; how he suffered and died for us. Ask Jesus to grant
his peace. Ask all the saints to lead that person home. Ask
forgiveness for the times you have missed a funeral or failed
to give comfort to families of the deceased. Rise slowly and
lift your arms. Imagine Jesus dancing for joy with his
beloved as he welcomes each one home.

The Spiritual Works of Mercy

Dominic: Dear friends, Christ also calls us to help one

another in spiritual matters. When we give ourselves to the spiritual works of mercy, we share in Christ's healing love. I will list these spiritual works here and suggest that you take them to prayer and design your own movement to extend Christ's healing love to the world.

> Christ calls us all:
> to admonish sinners,
> to instruct the ignorant,
> to counsel the doubtful,
> to comfort the sorrowful,
> to bear wrongs patiently,
> to forgive all injuries,
> to pray for the living and the dead.

Remember, friends, Jesus said he would know us by our actions. As you embody these corporal and spiritual works in your prayer life, may you also find ways to embody them in your everyday life.

Mary: Well said, my son. Our faith must never be simply a matter of private devotion. Love of God and love of neighbor can never be separated. My friends, draw upon the strength of your communities. When we gathered in the Upper Room to pray for the Spirit, we knew each other well and could therefore give personal support to one another. You need this today, as I needed it in my day. Our loving Creator never intended us to go it alone.

In my day, we went to the synagogue each week for common prayer, but every night we would gather in prayer as a family. Fathers and mothers would lead prayers of praise and blessing. Later we carried these same traditions over to our Christian gatherings. I lament the loss of this tradition. Too many families have no idea of the importance of praying with and for each other.

Ignatius: The Second Vatican Council reminds us that we are all called to holiness. All of us are called to share in the priesthood of Christ through our baptism.[11]

Mary: And how it fills me with joy when I see husbands blessing their wives and wives blessing their husbands! How I rejoice when I see parents blessing their children and children blessing their parents. We would have a very different sense of Church if Christians prayed and blessed their priests and priests, in turn, believed in the power of their priestly blessing. Children, I wish that you could see the grace that flows into the soul of your unborn child when mothers, fathers and children pray for that new addition to the family. Yes, we need to pray and bless one another to heal the wounds of sin.

Ignatius: Today, fellow pilgrims, there is a strong movement sweeping the Christian Churches that is directly inspired by the Holy Spirit. Christians are beginning to pray together, to study the Scriptures together, to share faith together. These gatherings are signs of God's speaking to your age and your culture.

Mary: Yes, beloved friends, as our retreat draws to a close, Dominic, Ignatius and I want to send you forth to share your faith. Remember that "we, who are many, are one body in Christ...."[12] We call you to celebrate this reality in flesh and bone, body, breath and Spirit. Walk with one another, bless one another, dance, sing and pray together. Pray with all God's gifts.

Dominic: And we thank you, dear ones, for choosing us as your mentors. We will not say good-bye, for we will be present to you for all time. We will continue to love you and lead you.

Ignatius: As we send you forth, we would like to lead you in a ritual of commissioning and anointing. This ritual is based on one of my favorite passages in Scripture, John 21:15-19. You may want to review it before we begin.

Here is a blessing, a commissioning that you retreatants can share in your homes and in your prayer groups. With this anointing, we call you all to "feed his sheep."

A Commissioning Anointing

This anointing holds tremendous power. All Christians by virtue of baptism may bless and pray for one another, using the signs and symbols that help us believe in the power of the Holy Spirit flowing through us.

Perhaps you would like some soft instrumental music. Ask each person in the assembly to choose a partner with whom to share this blessing. In the front of your gathering space (near a cross or an altar, if either is available), position several people who hold in their hands small bowls of scented holy oil[13] or holy water. Everyone in the assembly will both give the blessing to and receive the blessing from a partner.[14]

The first person, echoing Jesus' question to Peter, asks the other: "(Name), do you love Jesus?" The second person replies, "Yes, I do." Then the first anoints one hand of the other with oil, making the Sign of the Cross and saying: "Feed his lambs."

Again, the first person asks the second: "(Name), do you love Jesus?" and the second replies: "Yes, I do." Then the first anoints the other hand, again marking with the Sign of the Cross and saying: "Tend his sheep."

For the last time the first person asks the second: "(Name), do you love Jesus?" The second replies: "Yes, I do." This time, the first person anoints the forehead of the other with oil, making the Sign of the Cross and saying: "Feed his sheep." The person who has just received the blessing then rubs the oil into his or her palms, taking the anointing to heart. The two of them reverse roles and repeat the process.

When the first pair completes the prayer of anointing, the next pair should move forward to do the same until everyone who so desires has participated in this ritual. Finally, those holding the oil cups bless each other.

For Reflection

- How do I allow the Spirit to be the guiding force of my life?

- How often do I actually perform the corporal and spiritual works of mercy? In what ways has my retreat encouraged me to be more merciful?

- In what ways am I willing to change direction—give up an idea, give up a habit of sin—and dance in the joyful simplicity of the Lord?

Closing Prayer

Simple Gifts

Mary: In closing, dear retreatant friends, we would like to share with you one of our favorite dances, a final dance of celebration.

Dominic: This wonderful movement prayer, developed by the Shakers, is the oldest Christian liturgical dance in

North America. Perhaps you are familiar with the tune "Simple Gifts."

Ignatius: You can do this dance in a circle with a group of friends. It will give you a chance to embody all the lessons that we have learned in our seven days together.

Dominic: As you will discover, we begin by bowing our heads and shaking out our hands. As we do this, we cleanse our hearts and let go of all the fears and burdens that keep us away from the healing love of our Lord (Day Three).

Mary: In the second movement, we open our hands to God (Day One), and we reach out in trust, giving thanks and praise to the God of miracles (Day Two).

Ignatius: As we let go and open in trust, we also renew our walk with Christ (Day Four). First we step forward into the center of the circle, remembering our journey into the cave where God became flesh. Then we step backward, widening out God's circle of love to include all of humanity.

Mary: In the next movement, we step to the side and bow our heads, remembering how Christ humbled himself even to death—death on a cross (Day Five). As the song says, "When true simplicity is gained, to bow and to bend, we shan't be ashamed." So when we humble ourselves to become like Christ, we find that all our shame melts away. We become like little children, unafraid. We find joy and freedom in the simple gift of our bodies.

Ignatius: The song then leads us into celebration. And so we lift our arms and turn our hearts around, embodying the joy of Resurrection (Day Six).

Mary: Then we turn once more in a new direction, surrendering ourselves to God's Spirit and dancing in the divine love of our Lord (Day Seven).

Dominic: Dear pilgrims, we shall rejoice to see you and your friends dancing in the "valley of love and delight." Of course, you can also pray this dance by yourself, in which case you may like to imagine a circle of saints and loved ones dancing with you. Know that we will be in that circle with you!

Ignatius: Are you ready?

Mary: Let us pray.

Simple Gifts[15]

'Tis the **gift** *to be* **simple** / *'Tis the* **gift** *to be* **free**,...
> Take four steps forward toward the center of the circle on the accented words. As you walk, bend over slightly so you are looking at the ground and shake your hands toward it, one shake for each step. Cleanse your heart, shaking out all your tension, all your frustrations, all the sins of your soul.

'Tis the **gift** *to* **come** *down* / **where** *you ought to be....*
> Lift your arms, hands and face to the sky. Take in from God all the goodness, joy and love you need to sustain you as you take four steps backward, retracing your path to the circle's edge.

1

'Tis a gift   to be simple,   'tis a gift   to be free,

2

'tis a gift   to come down   where   we ought to be.

3

And when we   find ourselves   in a place   just right

4

'twill be   in the valley   of   love and delight.

5

When   true   simplicity   is gained,   to bow   and to bend   we shan't   be ashamed.

6

To turn,   turn,   will be our delight,   till by turning,   turning   we come around   right.

*And **when** we find **ourselves** / in the **place** just **right**,...*
>   Repeat the first motion, taking four steps forward while
>   bending your upper body toward the ground. Shake out all
>   your fears and worries, all that is not of God.

*'Twill **be** in the **valley** of **love** and **delight**....*
>   Take four steps back again, sharing the love you receive with
>   all those around you. Place your palms together, fingers
>   pointing to the sky.

When...
>   Take a step to the side with your right foot.

...true...
>   Bring your left foot to meet the right.

...simplicity...
>   Bend your knees and make a small bow with your head and
>   shoulders.

...is gained,...
>   Stand up straight again.

*To **bow** and to **bend**...*
>   Step to the left and close with your right foot.

*...we **shan't**...*
>   Bow your head, bending your knees.

*...be **ashamed**....*
>   Come up straight.

To turn, turn, will be our delight...
>   The Hebrew word for reconciliation *literally means to turn
>   our hearts around*. Lift your hands up and turn your body
>   to the right for one complete circle.

'Till by turning, turning we come round...
>   Now turn to your left, making another complete circle,
>   celebrating in the Spirit.

...right.

With palms together, bend your knees and bow your head,
to the Lord of our daring, our dreams and our dancing.

Ignatius: Now, dear retreatant friends, let us finish as we began—by signing ourselves with the cross of Christ's love.

All: In the name of the Father, and of the Son, and of the Holy Spirit....

Ignatius: Now, bring your hands together in a unity that is blessed, as we pray:

Mary: Amen to the God beyond us, the God of power and wonder, mystery and surprise, more immense than the universe, more vast than the sky!

Dominic: Amen to the God who lives among us, who creates community, who reconciles our differences, who calls us to be Church!

Ignatius: Amen to the God who dwells within us, in the heart cave, in the secrecy of our very soul!

Mary: It is in the name of this God who breathes life in us body and soul that we sign ourselves this day. Amen, beloved ones. Go in peace.

Notes

---

[1] Based on the parable "Vigilance" in *One Minute Wisdom* by

Anthony de Mello (Garden City, N.Y.: Doubleday, 1986), p. 11.

[2] John 16:21.

[3] See Exodus 19:4.

[4] Exodus 19:6b.

[5] See Exodus 34:29-35.

[6] See Genesis 1:1-2; 2:7.

[7] See Ezekiel 37:1-14.

[8] Found in *Laughter, Silence and Shouting: An Anthology of Women's Prayers*, compiled by Kathy Keay (London: HarperCollins, 1984), p. 93.

[9] Adapted from the *Spiritual Exercises of St. Ignatius*, trans. Louis J. Puhl, S.J. (Chicago: Loyola University Press, 1951).

[10] This traditional list of charitable actions by which we come to the aid of our neighbor is based on Matthew 25:31-46.

[11] See *The Constitution on the Church*, #40.

[12] Romans 12:5.

[13] See Day Six, page 144.

[14] It is also possible to have a group of three perform the blessing. Simply have the first person bless the second person and the second person bless the third. The third person then blesses the first. Thus the dynamic of each giving and receiving the blessing is maintained.

[15] This traditional dance of the Shakers was taught to us by Carla De Sola, and later adapted by Tria Thompson. The recorded song, "Simple Gifts," along with a complete explanation of the dance is available from St. Anthony Messenger Press in the collection *Full Body Blessing: Praying With Movement* by Betsey Beckman, Michael Sparough, S.J., and Bobby Fisher (1615 Republic St., Cincinnati, OH 45210).

Deepening Your Acquaintance

With Our Lady

Buby, Bertrand, S.M. *Mary of Galilee*. New York: Alba House, 1994.

Daino, Peter. *Mary, Mother of Sorrows, Mother of Defiance*. New York: Orbis Books, 1993.

Houselander, Caryll. *The Reed of God*. London: Sheed and Ward, 1944.

Johnson, Ann. *Miryam of Jerusalem*. Notre Dame, Ind.: Ave Maria Press, 1991.

_____. *Miryam of Judah*. Notre Dame, Ind.: Ave Maria Press, 1987.

_____. *Miryam of Nazareth*. Notre Dame, Ind.: Ave Maria Press, 1984.

McKenna, Megan. *Mary, Shadow of Grace*. New York: Orbis Books, 1995.

Noone, Patricia. *Mary for Today*. Chicago: Thomas More Press, 1977.

With Dominic

Englebert, Omar. *The Life of the Saints*, trans. Christopher and Anne Fremantle. New York: David McKay

Company, Inc., 1951.

Mandonnet, Pierre, O.P. *St. Dominic and His Work,* trans. Sister Mary Benedicta Larken, O.P. St. Louis: B. Herder Book Company, 1945.

Monshau, Michael, O.P. *Praying With Dominic,* Companions for the Journey series. Winona, Minn.: Saint Mary's Press, Christian Brothers Publications, 1993.

Tugwell, Simon, O.P. *The Way of the Preacher.* Springfield, Ill.: Templegate Publishers, 1979.

Vicaire, Marie-Humbert, O.P. *The Genius of St. Dominic: A Collection of Study Essays,* ed. Peter Lobo, O.P. Nagpur, India: Dominican Publications, 1981.

Vicaire, M. H., O.P. *St. Dominic and His Times,* trans. Kathleen Pond. Green Bay, Wis.: Alt Publishing Company, 1964.

With Ignatius

Bergan, Jacqueline Syrup and Marie Schwan. *Praying with Ignatius of Loyola,* Companions for the Journey series. Winona, Minn.: Saint Mary's Press, 1991.

Ganss, George E., S.J., ed. *Ignatius of Loyola: Spiritual Exercises and Selected Works,* Classics of Western Spirituality series. Mahwah, N.J.: Paulist Press, 1991.

Idigoras, Jose Ignacio Tellechea. *Ignatius of Loyola, The Pilgrim Saint,* trans. and ed. Cornelius Michael Buckley, S.J. Chicago, Ill.: Loyola University Press, 1994.

Link, Mark, S.J. *Challenge 2000, A Daily Meditation Program Based on the Spiritual Exercises of St. Ignatius* (Allen, Tex.:

Tabor Publishing, 1993).

O'Malley, John W. *The First Jesuits*. Cambridge, Mass.: Harvard University Press, 1993.

St. Ignatius' Own Story As Told to Luis Gonzalez With a Sampling of His Letters, trans. from Spanish William J. Young, S.J. Chicago: Loyola University Press, 1980.

The Spiritual Exercises of St. Ignatius; A Literal Translation and A Contemporary Reading, trans. David L. Fleming, S.J. St. Louis: The Institute of Jesuit Sources, 1978.

With Body Prayer and Movement

Audiocassettes

The Body at Eucharist: Gesture and Posture, by J. Michael Sparough, S.J., and Betsey Beckman. Music by Bobby Fisher. Cincinnati, Ohio: St. Anthony Messenger Press, 1990.

The Body at Eucharist: Senses and Symbols, by J. Michael Sparough, S.J., and Betsey Beckman. Music by Bobby Fisher. Cincinnati, Ohio: St. Anthony Messenger Press, 1990.

The Body at Prayer: Guided Meditations Using Gesture, Posture and Breath, With Original Music for Prayer, by J. Michael Sparough, S.J. Music by Bobby Fisher. Cincinnati, Ohio: St. Anthony Messenger Press, 1987.

The Body at Prayer II: Guided Meditations Using Gesture, Posture and Breath, With Original Music for Prayer, by J. Michael Sparough, S.J. Music by Bobby Fisher. Cincinnati, Ohio: St. Anthony Messenger Press, 1987.

Full Body Blessing: Praying With Movement, by J. Michael

Sparough, S.J., and Betsey Beckman. Music by Bobby Fisher. Cincinnati, Ohio: St. Anthony Messenger Press, 1992.

Treasures of the Heart: Meditations With Mary, Our Mother of Mercy, by J. Michael Sparough, S.J., and Betsey Beckman. Music by Bobby Fisher. Cincinnati, Ohio: St. Anthony Messenger Press, 1994.

Video

The Dancing Church, by Thomas Kane. Mahwah, N.J.: Paulist Press, 1991.

Books

Clarke, Mary and Clement Crist. *The History of the Dance*. New York: Crown Publishers, Inc., 1981.

Fisher, Constance. *Dancing the Old Testament*. Richmond, Calif.: The Sharing Company, 1980.

Kraus, Richard. *History of the Dance in Art and Education*. Englewood Cliffs, N.J.: Prentice Hall, Inc., 1969.

Roth, Nancy. *The Breath of God: An Approach to Prayer*. Cambridge, Mass.: Cowley Publications, 1990.

Schroeder, Celeste Snowber. *Embodied Prayer*. Liguori, Mo.: Triumph Books, 1995.

Sendry, Alfred and Mildred Norton. *David's Harp: The Story of Music in Biblical Times*. New York: The New American Library, 1964.

For a checklist of current dance and religion publications, contact The Sharing Company, 6226 Bernhard Ave., Richmond, CA 94805.